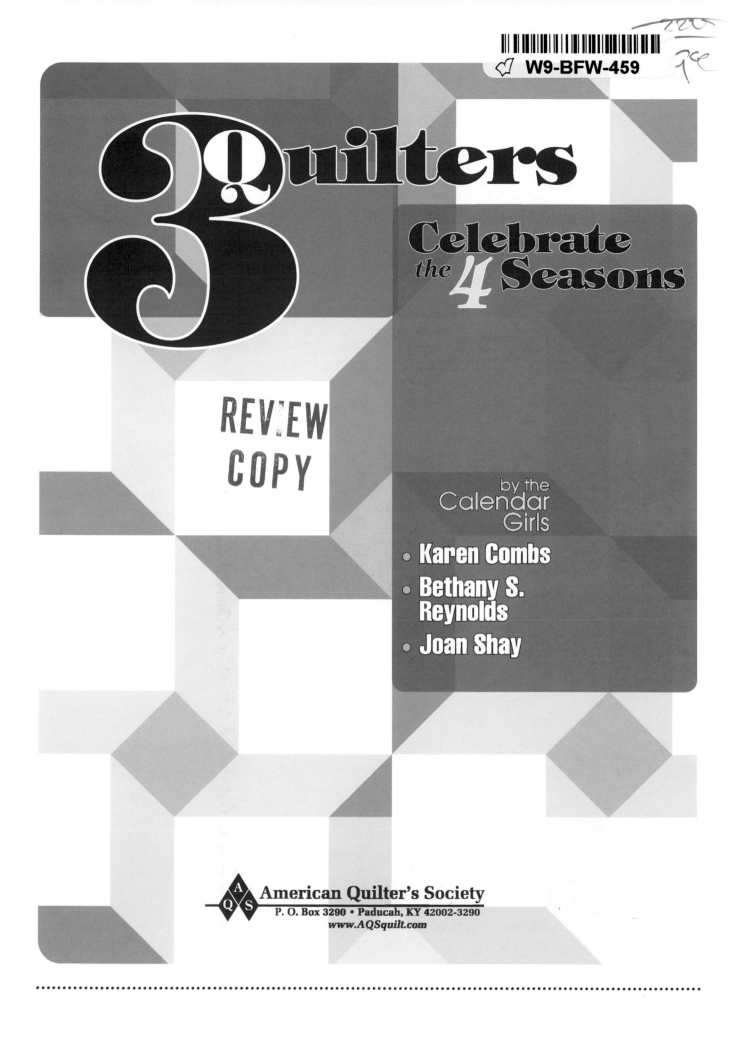

3 Quilters

Celebrate the 4 Seasons

by the Calendar Girls

- **Karen Combs**
- **Bethany S. Reynolds**
- **Joan Shay**

American Quilter's Society
P. O. Box 3290 • Paducah, KY 42002-3290
www.AQSquilt.com

Located in Paducah, Kentucky, the American Quilter's Society (AQS) is dedicated to promoting the accomplishments of today's quilters. Through its publications and events, AQS strives to honor today's quiltmakers and their work and to inspire future creativity and innovation in quiltmaking.

EDITOR: TERI COFFMAN
GRAPHIC DESIGN: ELAINE WILSON
COVER DESIGN: MICHAEL BUCKINGHAM
QUILT PHOTOGRAPHY: CHARLES R. LYNCH
HOW-TO ILLUSTRATIONS: KAREN COMBS AND BETHANY S. REYNOLDS
HOW-TO PHOTOGRAPHY: WILLIAM W. AND BETHANY S. REYNOLDS

Library of Congress Cataloging-in-Publication Data
Combs, Karen
    3 quilters celebrate the 4 seasons : by the calendar girls / By Karen Combs,
Bethany S. Reynolds, and Joan Shay
        p. cm.
    Includes bibliographical references
    ISBN 1-57432-838-7
   1. Patchwork--Patterns. 2. Quilting--Patterns. 3. Seasons in art. I. Reynolds,
Bethany S. II Shay, Joan. III. American Quilter's Society. IV. Title.
    TT835.C6482 2004
    746.46'041--dc22
                        2004001229

Additional copies of this book may be ordered from the American Quilter's Society, PO Box 3290, Paducah, KY 42002-3290; 800-626-5420 (orders only please); or online at www.AQSquilt.com. For all other inquiries, call 270-898-7903.

Some people come into our lives
and quietly go.
Others stay for awhile
and leave footprints on our hearts
and we are never the same.

anonymous

This book is dedicated to the many friendships that we have made as we travel the quilt world. To the students, teachers, and advisors who have changed our lives forever, we thank you.
Bethany, Karen, and Joan

Acknowledgments

From Joan:

None of this would have been possible without my wonderful friends and family. I am truly blessed. My deepest gratitude goes to them and especially to…

my husband, Tony — without his support and encouragement I would not be living my dream;

my children, Matthew, Kristin, her husband, Jon, and my two grandchildren, Shay and Sean, for enriching my life;

my mother, Barbara Moore (Petal Play South), for her love and assistance;

Judy Irish, a true artist whose machine quilting has greatly enhanced my quilts; and

Nan Berg and Liz Philbrook for assisting me in all our endeavors.

From Bethany:

To my husband, business partner, photographer, and best friend, Bill, and to my extraordinary son, Samuel — all my love and gratitude.

From Karen:

There are many people who supported and gave me encouragement while I wrote this book. I'd like to thank them in a special way. To…

my husband, Rick. Without your love, encouragement, patience, and the occasional "Go get 'em," I would not have my dream job.

my children, Angela and Josh, whose support and love mean the world to me. You both have grown to be wonderful young adults. I'm so proud of you!

Barbie Kanta and Judy Irish, whose machine quilting made my quilts shine. Thank you so much!

From all of us to…

Jeannie Sullivan, for bringing a ray of sunshine into our lives;

Barbara Smith, whose editing skills and guidance make this project easier;

Helen Squire, thank you for your dedicated efforts on our behalf; and

Bill and Meredith Schroeder and many others at the American Quilter's Society for allowing three friends to combine their unique talents and to have fun while doing it.

Many companies have supplied products for this book. Special thanks are extended to…

American & Efird, Inc., and Marci Brier for Mettler® and Signature® threads;

Blank Textiles and Clearwater Fabrics for the fabric and to Bruce Magidson, Renee Burdette, and Billy Alper for their help, friendship, and going the extra mile for us;

Hoffman California Fabrics, Robert Kaufman Fine Fabrics, Northcott Silk Inc., and FreeSpirit Fabrics for fabric;

J.T. Trading Corporation for basting spray and batting;

Pfaff American Sales for the Pfaff sewing machines used by Karen and Bethany;

Prym Dritz for notions and for Omnigrid® rotary cutters, rulers, and mats; and

Superior Threads and Heather Purcell for thread.

Contents

Introduction

Many months ago, during a short, cramped carpool ride between our hotel in Houston and the convention center where the International Quilt Festival is held each year, one of us suggested we write a book together. This idea met with immediate and enthusiastic agreement. We were all seasoned authors and designers, and we were already becoming fast friends. By the time we reached the convention center, a concept and an outline had been scribbled down on scrap paper. We even had a nickname and a theme song — "The Calendar Girls." We knew we could do this, and we couldn't wait to get started!

After we calmed down enough to think rationally, practical concerns arose. How were we going to combine our diverse styles? Would we try to do "Appli-bonded Stack-n-Whack Quilts of Illusion"? Or would we each do our own designs and trust the fantastic staff at the American Quilter's Society to pull everything together? We decided to steer a middle course. We would each be responsible for the projects for four months. These projects would showcase our individual areas of expertise. At the same time, we agreed to learn more about each other's techniques and incorporate them into our own designs whenever we could. Exploring the possibilities of this "cross-pollination" has been a great opportunity to stretch our design muscles and has kept our creative energy flowing throughout this project. In some cases, we found we could combine techniques in a single project. For other projects, we could offer a second version of the main project, showing two different approaches to the design. And we couldn't resist the challenge of combining all our talents to make one quilt, FORGET-ME-KNOTS.

Collaborating on designing and writing this book has been a new and wonderful experience for us. Each of us contributed our individual knowledge and skills, and we learned so much from each other. You will add your own unique quilt experiences as you create these projects. Our hope is that you will have as much fun making them as we had designing them for you. Perhaps you'll try one with a friend. You will strengthen your friendship as you share your skills. And remember, friendships, like quilts, are always in season!

Part One

Getting Started

This book is written using several techniques: Joan's Appli-Bond, Bethany's Stack-n-Whack, and Karen's Quilts of Illusion and Combing Through Your Scraps. Some of the quilts use one method. Other quilts combine several of the methods. Before starting a quilt from the pattern section of the book, here is information that will familiarize you with their different techniques:

Appli-bond is a unique three-dimensional appliqué technique. It is quick and easy because turning and sewing edges are eliminated. Two layers of fabric are bonded together and the design is cut on the line with no seam allowance. When the fabric is properly bonded, it will not fray even when washed and dried, and the pieces may be curled and shaped for added dimension.

Quilts of Illusion contain some sort of illusion. They may contain the illusion of depth or the illusion of motion by piecing and value placement, or they may contain the illusion of transparency by color and value selections. All are fun to make and intriguing to view.

The **Stack-n-Whack**® method is an easy way to create blocks with unique kaleidoscope designs. These designs require a set of identical pieces cut from a print fabric. Rather than finding and cutting each piece individually, a quilter can cut and layer a number of large, identical pieces of print rectangles to make a stack. Each piece cut from the stack produces a block kit, a set of identical pieces that will create the kaleidoscope effect for one block.

In the following sections, you will find detailed information about these techniques as well as fabric selection, color, and value.

FABRIC SELECTION

Selecting fabric for a quilt is always exciting and sometimes challenging. The first part of this chapter provides excellent information about selecting fabric for quilts in general. However, since this book is written by three different quilters with three very different styles, specific information has been added. Choosing fabric for an Appli-bond quilt or a Stack-n-Whack quilt is different than selecting fabric for a Quilt of Illusion. Review the suggestions for these special techniques before selecting fabric for your quilt.

Color

Color is important to a quilt—it can promote a feeling, set a mood, or express a season. Because these quilts are based on the seasons, you may wish to use the colors suggested within each pattern. If you decide to change colors, keep in mind that color will express a season, mood, or feeling. To reflect a season, use the suggestions below. Of course, you can always change the colors to match a room or just use colors you enjoy.

COLORS THAT REFLECT THE SEASONS

Winter (Plate 1): cool, dramatic colors ranging from jewel colors to dramatic black and white. Icy colors such as pure white, icy gray, icy blue, and violet also suggest winter. Christmas colors can also be used: vivid cranberry red and pine green are popular. Also, think of deeper, brighter colors that you see in the winter.

Spring (Plate 2): warm, clear colors: coral pinks, peach, poppy red, golden brown, greens, and aqua. Think of the vibrancy of a spring bouquet—yellow, pink, periwinkle blue, coral, and fresh greens, the emergence of a new leaf that is a bright yellow-green.

Plate 1. Winter colors: icy and dramatic

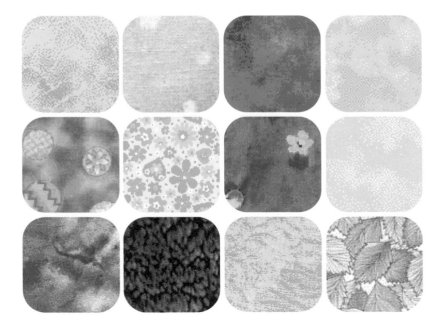

Plate 2. Spring colors: warm and clear

Summer (Plate 3): cool, gentle colors, slightly muted, ranging from pastel pinks, blues, and lavenders to deep dusty shades of plum, fuchsia, spruce, and watermelon red. In the summer, the colors are softened by the heat and are never sharp or harsh.

Autumn (Plate 4): warm, rich tones: coppery reds, tawny peach, and the earthy shades of green, brown, terra cotta, and jade green. These colors should always have a rich quality and be deeper, brighter colors.

COLOR TEMPERATURE

Colors are either warm or cool. Warm colors are the colors you see in fire: yellow, yellow-orange, orange, red-orange, and red (Plate 5). Warm colors are stimulating and they visually advance.

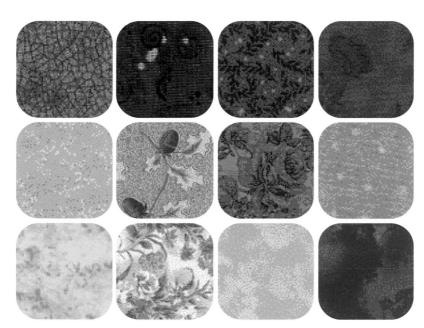

Plate 3. Summer colors: cool and gentle

Plate 5. Warm colors visually advance.

Cool colors are the colors you see in water: blue, blue-green, green, violet, and blue-violet (Plate 6). Cool colors are calming and visually recede.

Plate 6. Cool colors visually recede.

If you want to make an exciting quilt, use warm colors or very bright colors. COUNTERPOINT STARS (page 86) combines warm, bright colors (red and white) with a red/white/blue print and a deep blue that are lively and reminiscent of the Fourth of July holiday. If you want a quilt that is calmer, use cool colors or dulled colors.

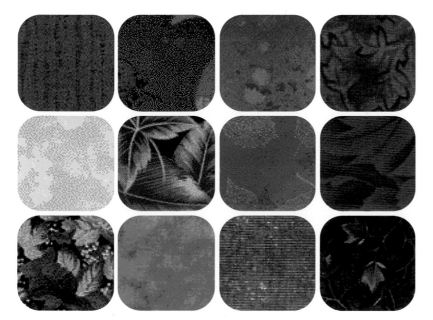

Plate 4. Autumn colors: warm and rich

Getting Started

Of course, many quilts use a combination of warm and cool colors. AUTUMN GLOW (page 105) is a combination of warm colors (red) and cool colors (green, blue) and is a rich blend of the colors you see in a fall landscape.

As you select colors for your quilt, remember the mood that warm and cool colors can suggest.

Scale

Scale or visual texture is very important to quilts. With too little texture, quilts may appear flat and uninteresting. Too much visual texture may detract from the graphic appeal of the quilt.

BUSY PRINTS

These prints have many colors and/or strong contrast within the print (Plate 7). They may be large or small in scale. Scrap quilts are an excellent place to use busy prints, especially smaller-scale prints. Stack-n-Whack designs work best with medium- to large-scale busy prints. Examples include BUNDLE UP (page 30), SWEET HEARTS (page 39), NOSEGAYS FOR MOTHER (page 68), COUNTERPOINT STARS (page 86), and DANCING LEAVES (page 111).

NONBUSY PRINTS

These prints generally have low contrast, fewer colors, and more subtle patterns (Plate 8). From a distance, these prints often appear as a solid color. However, they can add more depth and richness to a quilt than a flat, solid color fabric. Quilts of Illusion need prints that are not busy. They work best with subtle or tone-on-tone fabrics. Examples of these quilts are the SWEET HEARTS runner (page 45), SUMMER STAR (page 80), AUTUMN GLOW (page 105), and the DANCING LEAVES wall quilt (page 117).

Appli-bond quilts work well with both types of fabrics. Large- or medium-scale prints are used in the border and tone-on-tone prints or batiks are used in the background and flowers. Examples of these quilts are BUNDLE UP (page 30), ROCKIN' ROBIN (page 47), SPRING IS IN THE AIR (page 58), NOSEGAYS FOR MOTHER (page 68), BY THE SEA (page 94), THANKSGIVING BASKET (page 120), and PIECEFUL HOLIDAYS (page 127).

Some quilts, such as scrap quilts, can use a variety of textures. Large-, medium-, and small-scale prints all give a visual texture to the quilt.

Plate 7. Busy prints

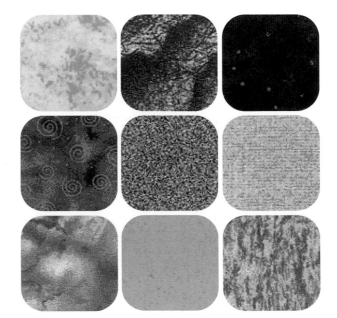

Plate 8. Nonbusy prints

In fact, the more fabrics that are used in a scrap quilt, the richer the quilt will look. An example of this type of quilt is DANCING LEAVES (page 111), which has a scrappy background.

When selecting fabric, check the pattern to see which type of fabric will work best for your quilt. If the pattern calls for a tone-on-tone print, do not substitute a busy print. You will not be happy with the result.

Value

Color is the first thing a quilter thinks about when selecting fabric. You may find yourself agonizing over the colors for a quilt. You may ask yourself, "Does this blue go with that red? Can yellow be added to the quilt?" Color can be intimidating! But, you may be surprised to learn that value and texture are more important than color. Surprising, isn't it! In most quilts, color gets all the credit while value and texture do all the work.

WHAT IS VALUE?

Right now, you may be asking, "What exactly is value?" Value is the lightness and darkness of a fabric, not how much you paid for it at the store! Quilts need light, medium, and dark values to create an exciting design. If the quilt does not have different values, the design may be boring. Quilts will vary in their value needs. Some will need medium and light values; some, light and dark values; and others, a variety of values.

For example, the three-dimensional hearts in SWEET HEARTS (page 39) use light, medium, and dark values. THANKSGIVING BASKET (page 120) is a scrap quilt that uses light and dark values. ROCKIN' ROBIN (page 47), an Appli-bond quilt, uses a variety of values. Check the pattern for each quilt to determine the values you need.

Many quilters are unsure about value and stick with medium values. While this may feel safe, it does not make for an exciting design.

Some quilters may be afraid of value because they are unsure whether a fabric is light, medium, or dark. It may seem confusing, but it does not have to be. There are a few tricks to help you determine the value of a fabric.

HOW TO DETERMINE VALUE

Remember, the value of the fabric refers to the lightness or darkness of a fabric. Many times, value is relative to its neighboring fabrics. This demonstration will help you understand how value is determined.

When this fabric is looked at alone, it appears light (Plate 9). However, when a lighter fabric is placed next to it, the fabric now appears darker (Plate 10). When a very dark fabric is laid next to the first fabric, it appears lighter again (Plate 11).

Plate 9. Medium fabric appears light in value.

Plate 10. Medium fabric now appears darker when a lighter fabric is placed next to it.

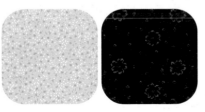

Plate 11. Medium fabric now appears light when a darker fabric is placed next to it.

You may ask yourself, "What happened? Is it magic? Why did the fabric's value change?" Because value is relative, you can change a fabric's value by surrounding it by different values. A fabric's neighbors can influence its value. You can make a medium fabric look light by placing a dark fabric next to it or make it look dark by placing a light fabric near it (Plate 12).

Plate 12. Medium fabric appears medium when it is surrounded by a light and a dark fabric.

However, some fabrics will always be a light or a dark. An off-white, white, light gray, and light tan will look light, no matter what fabric surrounds it (Plate 13). Dark fabrics are dark, no matter what other fabrics surround them (Plate 14). Medium fabrics can swing between light and dark, depending on the fabric that surrounds them (Plate 15).

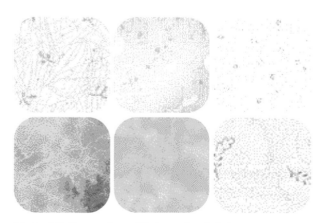

Plate 13. Examples of light value fabrics

As you can see, the value of the fabric can depend on the fabric that surrounds it as well as its own lightness or darkness. You may wish to use a Value Viewer tool to help you select fabrics (see Supplies and Resources on page 142).

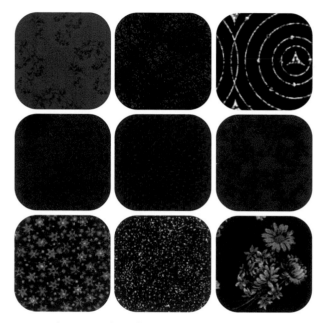

Plate 14. Examples of dark value fabrics

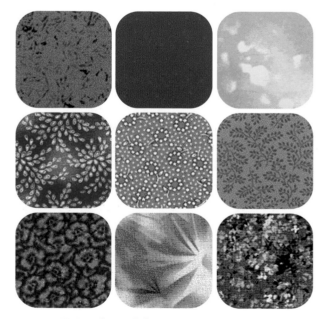

Plate 15. Medium fabrics can appear as light or dark values.

FABRIC SELECTION TIPS
Quilts of Illusion

Transparency is the illusion of layers that you can see through. It is as if you have taken one piece of fabric, laid another fabric over part of it, but you can still see through to the bottom fabric (Plate 16). AUTUMN GLOW (page 105) has the illusions both of transparency and motion. By using the right color and value, the shapes appear to overlap, but are also transparent. Transparency is a magical illusion that can give an intricate look to your patchwork. The illusion of motion is created by using diagonal patchwork lines rather than vertical and horizontal lines. The diagonal lines lead your eye around the surface of the quilt, creating the impression or the illusion of movement to the quilt.

The illusion of depth as in the three-dimensional SWEET HEARTS (page 39) is also a magical illusion (Plates 17 and 18). The blocks appear to have shape, and it's hard to believe they are really flat.

When selecting fabric for Quilts of Illusion, there are a few guidelines about value and texture you need to follow.

VALUE IN ILLUSIONS

Pay particular attention to the fabric value suggested in the pattern. This will aid you in creating a transparent or three-dimensional effect. If the pattern calls for a medium blue, do not substitute a light blue. Instead, use a medium blue or another medium color. The value and its placement create the illusion. If the values are changed, you will not have the transparent or the three-dimensional effect.

The heart in Plate 19 uses the same value and the illusion of depth is not strong. However, when a darker value is added to the heart sides in Plate 20, page 14, the illusion of depth becomes clear.

Plate 16. With the right color and value, the illusion of transparency appears.

Plate 17. This heart is not three-dimensional.

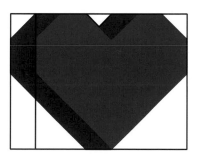

Plate 18. By adding a dark value and more lines, this heart becomes three-dimensional.

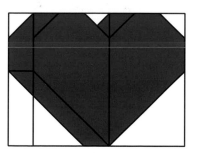

Plate 19. All are the same value with no depth.

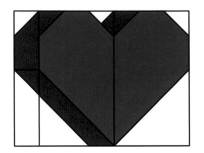

Plate 20. Darker value is added, depth appears.

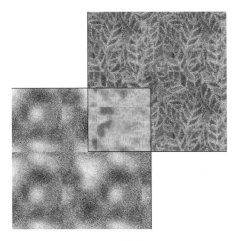

Plate 21. No transparency, all the same value.

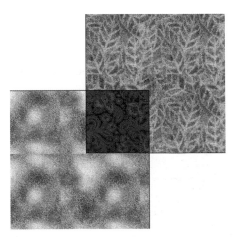

Plate 22. Dark blue is added, transparency appears.

With the illusion of transparency, the correct values must also be used in order for the illusion to be seen. In Plate 21, the values are all the same and the illusion of transparency does not show. However, in Plate 22, when a dark blue is placed in the center square, the illusion appears. A dark green would work as well.

When selecting fabrics, always use the fabrics suggested in the quilt pattern as your guide for value.

TEXTURE IN ILLUSIONS

For quilts with the illusion of transparency, such as in COUNTERPOINT STARS (page 91), use nonbusy prints (explained on page 10). Tone-on-tone fabrics work the best.

The three-dimensional designs of the SWEET HEARTS (page 39) have both busy and nonbusy textures (explained on page 10). A busy print is used in the heart portion and a nonbusy print is used in the sides.

In the SWEET HEARTS runner (page 45), nonbusy prints are used both in the heart as well as the sides of the heart.

To give you the best results for each project, study the quilt photograph for the type of texture to use.

Scrap Quilts

Scrap quilts are a favorite of many quilters. For the best results, use a variety of fabrics. The more you use, the better the scrap quilt will look. Select a variety of light and dark values and a variety of colors and prints. See Thanksgiving Basket (page 120) for an example of using an assortment of light scraps in the background and dark scraps in the basket. If you are not sure about selecting value, reread the Value section on pages 11–12.

Appli-bond Quilts

When you are making an appliqué quilt, two types of fabrics are needed: background fabric and fabric for the appliqué. In selecting your fabrics, choose 100 percent cotton. Other types of fabrics may not hold a sharp crease, and they are more likely to fray. Purchase fabrics with a high thread count and avoid any loose weaves, which will fray.

Background fabrics need not be limited to white or ecru. Be creative! You can use printed, multicolored, and hand-dyed fabrics. You might also consider muted plaids, pastels, or blacks. Dark backgrounds create a dramatic feel.

Unless you plan to wash the finished quilt, it's best not to prewash the fabrics. Prewashing removes the sizing applied by the manufacturer. This sizing helps to stabilize the appliqué pieces. If the fabrics are properly bonded, there will be no fraying and curled fabrics will stay curled (curling is explained on page 18).

Many quilters do not prewash, but you can do what suits your needs. You can still wash and dry these quilts after they have been made, even if the fabrics were not prewashed. However, it is important to check fabrics for bleeding before you use them. This can be done simply by cutting a small swatch of fabric and placing it in a clear glass of water for a few minutes. Let the fabric swatch dry on a white piece of similar fabric. If the white fabric is stained, the swatch fabric is unsuitable for that project.

The larger the variety of colors and shades you use, the more interesting the finished quilt will be.

Tone-on-tone or nonbusy prints (explained on page 10) add texture, and the shading adds to the realism. Hand-dyed gradations and batiks are also very effective for the shading.

Consider using the wrong sides of fabrics, which are generally a little lighter. Use solid colors sparingly. They can be boring if overused.

Bonding two different fabrics together adds interest. Remember that real flowers are generally darker in the center and gradually become lighter toward the edges, and that real flower petals and leaves are not the same shade on both sides. Your fabric petals can be different as well.

Stack-n-Whack Quilts
Main Fabric

Most medium- to large-scale prints will produce interesting Stack-n-Whack pieces. Small-scale prints can be effective if the pieces are also small. In general, choose a fabric with a repeat length that is longer than the piece you plan to cut. Look for prints with good contrast. Lively prints with a variety of shapes, lines, and colors make the most interesting blocks. Strong contrast or bright colors in the print will make bold kaleidoscope designs (Plate 23).

Plate 23. High-contrast prints can produce dramatic blocks.

If you prefer a quieter look, choose a print with medium contrast (Plate 24).

Plate 24. Medium-contrast prints would make understated blocks.

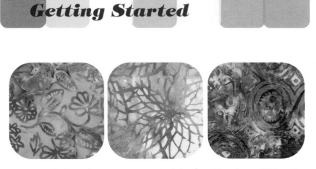

Plate 25. Batiks are not suitable for Stack-n-Whack.

Plate 26a. Fold the reverse side to the front to see how a fabric will work for the Magic Mirror-Image Trick.

Plate 26b. Detail

Hand-printed fabrics such as batiks (Plate 25) are not usually suitable for Stack-n-Whack. The design repeats are not as consistent as the repeats on commercial prints.

Special effects are possible with stripes and symmetrical prints. They can produce exciting designs if they are selectively cut. The BUNDLE UP quilt (page 30) shows how a stripe fabric can be used effectively.

The SWEET HEARTS wall quilt (page 39) and FORGET-ME-KNOTS (page 132) show a variation on the Stack-n-Whack technique, the Magic Mirror-Image Trick. In this method, the front and reverse sides of the fabric alternate to create a design in which the patterns on each side of a seam line form a mirror image. Prints that are well-saturated on the reverse side work best for this variation. To see how a fabric might be used with the Magic Mirror-Image Trick, fold the reverse side of the fabric back over the front side. Slide the edge over until you find the point where the pattern mirrors (Plate 26a). The type of image you see along the mirror-image line approximates the effect you will have at the seam line between two pieces (Plate 26b detail).

In order to purchase the correct amount of yardage for a Stack-n-Whack project, you will need to know the design repeat of the main fabric. See pages 21–22 for instructions on finding this measurement.

BACKGROUND AND ACCENT FABRICS

These fabrics should complement the main fabric without competing with it for attention. Watch out for distracting fabrics. If you suspect a print may be too busy, trust your judgment. Good choices include subtle, low-contrast fabrics with few colors, and monoprints or print solids (Plate 27). Mottled textural prints are always a safe choice. Light solids are also traditional favorites.

APPLI-BOND INSTRUCTIONS

The following section describes how to use fusing to make unique quilts that combine patchwork and three-dimensional Appli-bond appliqué. Supplies and techniques to attach the Appli-bond pieces to a quilt are also included.

Bonding the Fabric

It is essential that you use HeatnBond® Ultrahold Iron-on Adhesive as your bonding agent. It is an adhesive as opposed to a fusible web; therefore, you will not have fraying because the fibers will be glued together. The fact that it is an adhesive also allows you to curl and shape the pieces. You heat the piece, thus melting the glue. Shape it and hold it until it is cool. The glue hardens and the shape is retained. You must use the Ultrahold—you cannot curl or shape with a lighter product.

Here is some general information to help you when bonding fabrics:

❖ Iron the fabrics to be bonded. I do not pre-wash my fabrics. Test the fabric to see that it will not bleed as explained on page 15. To help eliminate wrinkles, spray the fabric with sizing.

❖ When considering fabric choices, there are three combinations you could use:
1. Wrong sides together
2. Right side to wrong side
3. Two different fabrics

Plate 27. Low-contrast fabrics work well for background and accent fabrics.

❖ Cut two pieces of fabric and one piece of HeatnBond the exact same size. If the fabric is cut larger than the bonding material, the edges will not be bonded. If the bonding material is larger than the fabric, you will have a mess on your ironing surface

❖ Set a dry iron on the cotton setting. Following the manufacturer's instructions, apply the bonding material to the wrong side of one of the two pieces of fabric. To keep the fabric from slipping during bonding, secure the bonding material to the fabric by placing the iron on several sections of the fabric for one or two seconds. To complete the bonding, move the iron in circles to prevent scorching the fabric or leaving vent marks from the iron. I find that I generally have to iron the fabric a little longer than recommended to get a good bond (six to eight seconds). It is easy to tell if you have bonded the fabric long enough. If the pieces are separating and you see that the surface inside shines, you have underbonded the piece and need to heat it longer. If the inside is very dull, you have overbonded it and you will need to start again.

❖ Bond large fabric pieces in sections to be sure each area is fused.

❖ Let the piece cool before you remove the paper backing. For easy paper removal, score it with a pin, fold along the scored line, then peel off the paper. After the paper has been removed, bond the two fabric pieces, wrong sides together.

❖ Trace your template on the bonded fabric and cut the desired number of pieces on the line leaving no seam allowance.

❖ Attach motifs according to the instructions given in the projects. If your needle

Plate 28. Shaping a sleeve for the NOSEGAY quilt (page 68)

Plate 29. Shaping a petal

becomes gummy from stitching through the bonded fabric, you can clean it up by wiping it with rubbing alcohol.

Curling and Shaping

Specific instructions for curling or shaping the motifs are given in each pattern. Generally, most pieces are curled after they are attached to the background. This allows you to shape it more accurately.

To curl a bonded piece, heat it with an iron and wrap it around an object to create the desired shape. A pen or a pencil (not one with 8 sides) will give you a tight curl (Plate 28). Shape it over your finger for a more gentle curl (Plate 29). Be careful. It will be hot. Pieces can also be "scrunched" or crimped by bunching the fabric slightly (Plate 30). Hold the piece in place until it is cool. If you are unhappy with the shape after curling it, iron it flat and recurl it.

"Fluffing" is not a very technical term, but it describes how many of the motifs such as the pom-poms in BUNDLE UP (page 30) are shaped. To fluff, simply place the iron on the completed motif and heat for two to three seconds. Then rub your hand back and forth over the motifs, thus fluffing the piece (Plate 31). This technique really adds dimension to motifs that have many pieces.

Supplies for Appli-bond

APPLI-BOND NEEDLES

When I first started doing Appli-bond appliqué, I attached the bonded pieces to the background by using an embroidery needle. This was often difficult, especially when stitching through several thicknesses. I have since discovered better needles. I call them Appli-bond needles. They have three very sharp cutting edges and easily pierce several layers of bonded fabric. The eye of the needle accommodates two strands of embroidery floss. A third strand can be added if you use a needle-threader. You won't want to use the needles for traditional appliqué as they are too sharp and will cut the fabric. These needles are also helpful when doing a buttonhole stitch around a fused shape as in fusible appliqué. See Supplies and Resources on page 142.

EMBROIDERY NEEDLES

An embroidery needle is used to embroider unbonded fabric. It has a long narrow eye that easily accommodates floss.

EMBROIDERY FLOSS

Embroidery floss has six strands per skein. Cut floss to a workable length, no longer than 18". Separate the strands by pulling one strand at a time, straight up and out of the skein. This eliminates twisting. When using multiple strands, always separate the strands first and then put them back together to increase the volume of the floss, making the stitches fuller. Each pattern instructs you on the number of strands necessary for a particular embroidery stitch. Combining two different shades of floss creates an interesting effect.

BEADS

Some designs call for French knots, which are really easy. You can, however, replace French knots with beads if you prefer. Some of the flowers in this book are embellished with beads, which really emphasize the texture.

Here are some things to remember when purchasing beading supplies:

♣ Use glass beads. Remember you will probably be ironing over them, and plastic beads will melt.

♣ Seed beads are very small beads that are perfect for the centers of flowers. Larger beads work well for the eyes of the birds and fish.

Plate 30. Crimping a leaf for the THANKSGIVING BASKET quilt (page 120)

Plate 31. Fluffing the ski cap pom-poms for the BUNDLE UP quilt on page 30

✤ Make sure your Appli-bond needle can fit through the opening of the bead.

✤ A ceramic bead dish, sold in bead stores, is helpful for handling small beads. Ceramic is preferable to plastic because plastic creates static.

✤ Nylon beading thread is recommended for attaching the beads because it is much stronger than regular thread and the beads do not cut it. I use size D.

Embroidery Techniques

FRENCH KNOTS

Many of the Appli-bond petals are attached with French knots, allowing the petals to remain free for a three-dimensional effect.

To make a French knot, use the number of strands of embroidery floss indicated and wrap the Appli-bond needle the suggested number of times. Bring the needle up through the fabric where you want the knot to be and wrap the thread around the needle the indicated number of times. Holding the thread taut, push the needle straight down through the fabric, close to where the thread first emerged but not in the same hole. Hold the wrap in place and pull the needle and thread completely through the fabric and thread wraps. Do not pull the thread too tight, as it will diminish the size of the knot (Fig. 1–1).

STEM STITCH

This stitch is used to embroider veins in the leaves. Use the number of strands of embroidery floss indicated in the pattern directions. Bring the Appli-bond needle up through the fabric, then down a stitch length away. Bring the needle to the top again in the middle of the previous stitch and pull the thread all the way through (Fig. 1–2).

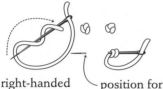

right-handed   position for 2nd knot

left-handed   position for 2nd knot

Fig. 1–1. French knot

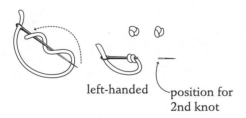

right-handed   left-handed

Fig. 1–2. Stem stitch

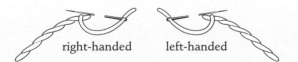

Stab Stitch. To make a stab stitch, bring the needle straight up through the fabric at A. Push the needle straight down through the fabric, a stitch away, at B.

STACK-N-WHACK INSTRUCTIONS

This section outlines the procedure for preparing (stacking) and cutting (whacking) the fabrics to make sets of identical pieces (block kits). Each block kit will have a unique design. While the number of layers to cut will vary depending on the design, the stacking process is the same for all projects.

Finding and Cutting the Layers

The repeats are cut from a single layer of fabric. In this book the stacks are cut from a half-width of fabric, which is generally 21"–22" wide. Begin by folding the fabric with selvages together to find the center, or, if the fabric is wider than 45", measure off 21" from one selvage. Cut or tear up along the lengthwise grain for about a yard. Fold the remaining fabric out of the way and square off the cut end of the fabric (Plate 32).

Switch the bulk of the fabric to your right if you are right-handed or to your left if you are left-handed. Smooth out the squared-off end of the fabric on your cutting mat. The length of the layers to cut for the stack depends on the design repeat length of the print. To determine the repeat length, find a motif along one selvage. Glance along the selvage until you find the same motif, in the same orientation. Measure between these two points to find the design repeat length. Check the Stack-n-Whack chart for your project to see in which category the lengthwise design repeat falls. The print in these photos has a repeat length of 11⅞" (Plate 33).

If the Stack-n-Whack chart for your project directs you to use just one repeat for each layer, you will use the length you have just measured for the length of the rectangle. If you need to use two or three repeats for each layer, count out that number of repeats and measure the total length. This length is the "magic number." It may be any-

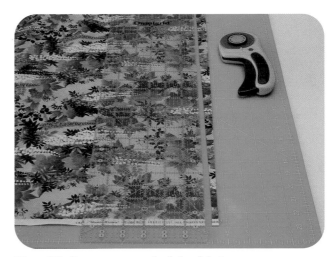

Plate 32. Square one end of the fabric.

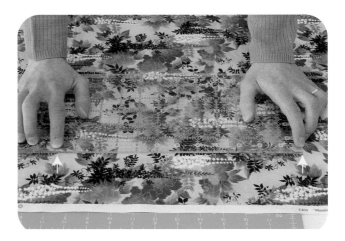

Plate 33. Measure the design repeat length.

Plate 34. Two repeats measure 23¾".

Plate 35. On both sides measure from the squared-off edge to the "magic number" and mark with cuts.

Plate 36. Line up your ruler with the cuts and cut across the fabric.

Plate 37. Use your fingers to align the design across the cut edge, which will nearly disappear as it lines up.

where from 6" to 36", depending on the print and the project. This number will be the length of the rectangle. For the print shown here, two repeats would measure 23¾" (Plate 34, page 21).

The following photos show a layer that is one repeat long. For the next step, ignore the print motifs. It no longer matters what part of the print you used as a reference to find the repeat length. Measure up from the straightened edge along the selvage side to the magic number. Mark the length with a 3"–4" rotary cut. Measure and cut again at the torn side (Plate 35).

Line up your ruler with the cut marks and cut across the width to make the first layer (Plate 36).

With selvages and cut edges aligned, lay the first rectangle on the remaining fabric so that the print matches. Smooth out the top layer and use your fingertips to match up the design all across the cut edge that is nearest to the remaining uncut fabric. The edge should nearly disappear as it lines up with the print on the lower, uncut layer. The other end of the rectangle does not need to match up precisely (Plate 37).

When you have the top layer matched, lay your ruler down along the edge and cut across (Plate 38).

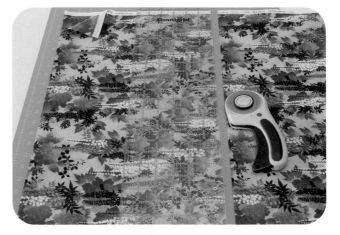

Plate 38. Cut the second layer along the matched edge.

You now have two identical print rectangles. Set the top piece aside. Cut or tear up along the length of the fabric, if necessary, and smooth out the portion you will be cutting. Use the second layer again to cut a third layer, and the remaining layers. The second layer will be the correct length, even if you have made a minor error in measuring or cutting the first layer. By using the second piece as a guide to cut the rest, you will not compound any errors. You will still be able to use the first layer in the stack, even if it is slightly shorter or longer than the others.

Repeat this process until you have the number of layers needed for the stack, as directed in the project instructions (Plate 39).

Plate 39. Continue using the second rectangle to cut the remaining layers.

Stacking the Layers

Press the layers one at a time to remove any wrinkles, pressing along the lengthwise grain to avoid distortion. If you have prewashed the fabric, it is a good idea to use a little sizing or spray starch to return some crispness to the fabric. This will make the pieces easier to handle and will help keep bias edges from stretching.

Stack up the layers, smoothing out each piece so that the selvages align. When you have all the layers stacked, use the following "stick-pinning" method to line up the motifs accurately through the layers. You'll need one pin with a large round head and several flower-head pins. These are long pins with a large flat head that will not interfere with the ruler. If you do not have these, you can use long pins with small metal heads. These are harder to see, though, so take extra care to keep stray pins out of the way of your cutting blade.

To "stick-pin" fabric layers, select a point on the fabric design about 1"–1½" from the crosswise (cut) edge. Look for something that's easy to spot, such as the tip of a leaf. Place the point of the round-headed pin on this spot (Plate 40, page 24).

Why am I using only the lengthwise repeats?

Be sure to cut all these layers from the same half of the fabric. Printing and finishing processes can cause slight distortions even in high-quality fabrics, and the differences may be noticeable in the finished blocks if you use crosswise, rather than lengthwise, repeats. You may also find that the crosswise repeats are staggered, so that they only match up for part of the width. This can result in a stack that is too narrow to cut enough block kits for the project.

Plate 40. Place the pin on a distinctive part of the design.

Plate 41. Push the pin through the same spot on all the layers.

Plate 42. Hold the pin and fabric layers tight. Pin through all the layers with a flower-head pin.

Lift the top layer of fabric, sliding the pin through. Find the same point on the next layer and slide the pin through (Plate 41). Continue lifting layers and pinning through this point until you have gone through all the layers

Slide the pin all the way through to the head and hold it in place with your thumb and forefinger. Hold the pin straight up and down and smooth out the surrounding fabric. Take a flower-head pin and pin across through all the layers, right beside the stick pin (Plate 42).

Remove the stick pin. Lay the fabric down flat and place flower-head pins at three other points across the width. For additional accuracy, also pin along the selvage and torn edge. Trim the stack along the pinned crosswise edge to ensure a straight edge through all the layers (Plate 43, page 25).

Turn the stack around or rotate the mat. Cut a strip through all the layers, using the strip width measurement given in the Stack-n-Whack chart for your project. To cut strips wider than your ruler, measure and cut at each side, as for the repeats (Plate 35 on page 22). Cut the strip into block kits as directed in your project's Stack-n-Whack chart. For more accurate cutting, re-pin the crosswise edge before cutting each additional strip.

Each block kit will produce a different design, as shown with 60° diamonds in Plate 44.

Making Additional Stacks

If the project requires a second stack, cut the stack from the remaining width of the fabric, starting with a new first layer. This stack should produce a new assortment of blocks. If the crosswise repeats line up side by side, trim an inch or two from the beginning of the fabric to offset the pattern before cutting the first layer.

ROTARY CUTTING

Here are some guidelines for rotary cutting the projects in this book. The instructions in this section are written for right-handed sewers. The illustrations show both right-handed and left-handed positions.

Most shapes used in these projects can be cut with any standard rotary cutting ruler or with a combination of a standard ruler and a temporary template. Some shapes are more easily cut with Bethany's Stack-n-Whack specialty rulers, which are noted in the pattern instructions. (See Supplies and Resources on page 142).

Cutting Strips

Unless otherwise directed in the instructions, begin with the fabric folded in half lengthwise, with selvages together. Trim the right end of the fabric to get a smooth edge, perpendicular to the fold. Cut a strip across the width, using the strip width measurement in your project directions. Cut additional strips as needed, taking care that the cuts remain perpendicular to the fold so the strips will be straight.

Unfold the strips. You can stack up several strips if desired. If the fabric has a directional print, take care to maintain the print orientation when placing the strips together.

For Stack-n-Whack block kits, the fabric should be unfolded and stacked with all layers right side up. Cut and stack the repeats, following the instructions on pages 21–24.

Cutting Unusual Shapes

Most of the projects in this book use common shapes such as squares, half-square triangles, and 45-degree diamonds. A few of the designs use less common shapes. Here are cutting directions for those shapes.

Plate 43. Pin along one cut edge and on each side. Then trim along the pinned crosswise edge.

Plate 44. Each Stack-n-Whack block will have a unique design.

CUTTING 45-DEGREE TRIANGLE WEDGES

Prepare the template on page 63 (triangle wedge) in one of the following ways:

Trace the guide as accurately as possible on clear template plastic. Cut out the plastic cutting guide. With clear tape, attach the cutting guide to the underside of your ruler, with the right edge of the guide aligned with the right edge of the ruler. Or, you can lay your ruler over the template with the right edge of the ruler on the right edge of the guide, and mark the guidelines on the ruler with a marker or tape. Use a permanent marker or a wet-erase marker so it doesn't rub off on your fabric (Fig.1–3).

Lay the ruler with the cutting guide down on the strip set, with the top and bottom edges of the guide aligned with the edges of the strip. Place the edge of the ruler far enough in to avoid the selvages. Cut along the edge through all layers. Set aside this first cut, which is scrap fabric (Fig. 1–4).

Carefully turn the strip set around so the angled edge is to your left. Lay the ruler down with the left edge of the cutting guide on the angled edge and cut. For additional wedges, slide the ruler and continue cutting double-triangles (Fig. 1–5).

Align the 45-degree line of your ruler with the cut edge of the piece and cut diagonally to make two 45-degree wedges (Figs. 1–6 and 1–7).

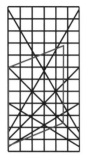 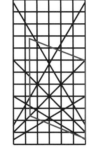

Fig. 1–3. Left-handed   Fig. 1–3. Right-handed

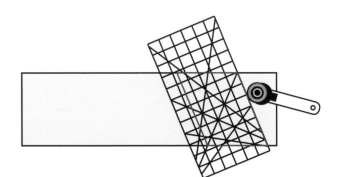

Fig. 1–4. Left-handed   Fig. 1–4. Right-handed

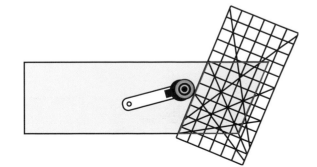 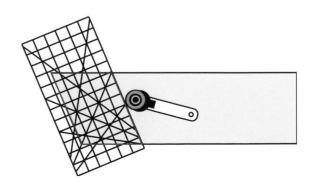

Fig. 1–5. Left-handed   Fig. 1–5. Right-handed

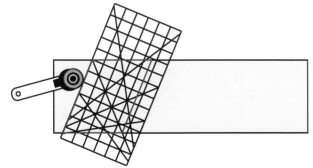

These wedges can also be cut using the Stack-n-Whack® 45° Triangle Tool (see Supplies and Resources on page 142). Follow the cutting instructions provided with the tool.

Cutting 60-Degree Diamonds

On the right end of the strip-set, lay the ruler down with the 60-degree line along one long edge. Because the placement of the 60-degree line varies on different brands of rulers, your ruler may be positioned differently from the one in the illustration. Place the edge of the ruler far enough in to avoid the selvages. Cut along the edge through all layers. Set aside this first cut, which is scrap fabric (Fig. 1–8).

Carefully turn the strip-set around so the angled edge is to your left. Place the line used to measure the strip width (in this example, 3") on the angled edge, and the 60-degree line on one straight edge. Cut to make the diamond (Fig. 1–9).

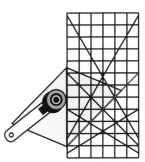

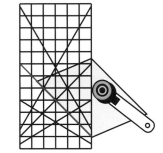

Fig. 1–6. Left-handed   Fig. 1–6. Right-handed

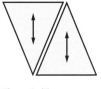

Fig. 1–7

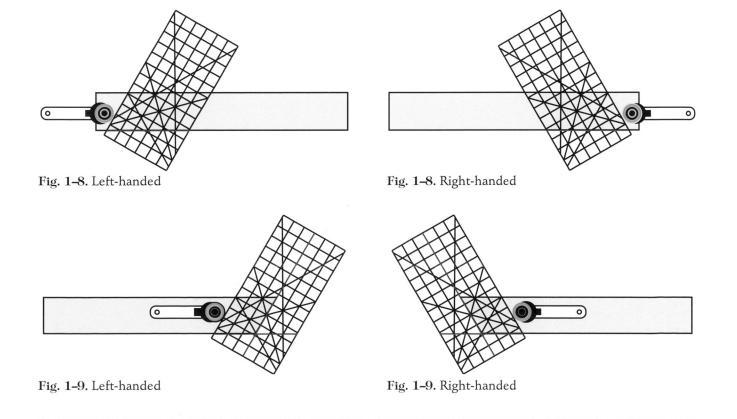

Fig. 1–8. Left-handed

Fig. 1–8. Right-handed

Fig. 1–9. Left-handed

Fig. 1–9. Right-handed

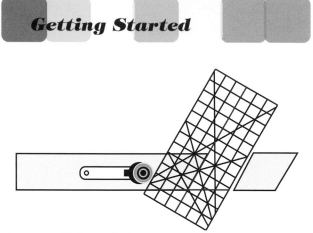

Fig. 1–10. Left-handed

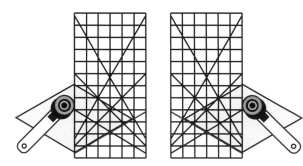

Fig. 1–11. Left-handed   **Fig. 1–11.** Right-handed

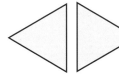

Fig. 1–12

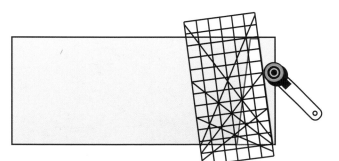

Fig. 1–13

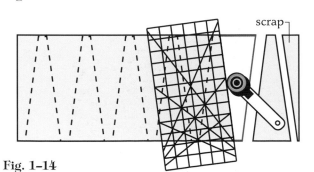

scrap

Fig. 1–14

Fig. 1–10. Right-handed

To cut additional diamonds, do not turn the strip. Slide the ruler along the long edge and line up the 60-degree line and the strip width measurement line for each cut (Fig. 1–10).

CUTTING 60-DEGREE TRIANGLES

Follow the directions for cutting 60-degree diamonds. Cut the diamond in half, using the 60-degree line along one edge for greater accuracy (Figs. 1–11 and 1–12).

CUTTING 15-DEGREE WEDGES

Prepare the template on page 37 (January pattern). To cut the fan wedges, place the wedge template at one end of the strip-set, lining up the short end with the strip edges. Use a ruler as a straightedge to protect the template, and cut along both long sides (Fig. 1–13).

Turn the template so the wider end is at the opposite edge, lining up the cut edges, and cut to make the next block kit. Continue along the strip, turning the template each time (Fig. 1–14).

Wedges can also be cut using the Stack-n-Whack® 15° Fan Ruler (see Supplies and Resources on page 142). Follow the cutting instructions provided with the ruler.

Part Two

The Projects

Bundle Up *by Bethany Reynolds*

These ski caps and mittens recall snowy childhood winters. The Stack-n-Whack cutting technique ensures that everyone gets a unique cap! Joan taught Bethany how to make the cute pom-poms with her Appli-bond technique.

Bundle Up

Before beginning, review the instructions for Stack-n-Whack on page 21 and for Appli-bond on page 17.

Fabric Requirements

Measurements are in yards unless otherwise indicated.

If the design repeat of the **Cap Fabric** is:	7"–10"	11"–14"	15"–17"	18"–26"	over 26"
You will need this many yards for the Stack-n-Whack blocks:	1⅜	1⅞	2¼	3¼	4 repeats

Additional Fabrics	
White – background	2¼
Blue, red, green, and purple – fabric for hat bands, pom poms, and mittens	⅜ each of 4 colors
Lengthwise stripe – border*	1⅝
Backing	3
Binding	½

* For fabrics with a repeat over 15", the Cap Fabric yardage includes the border. If you would like to use a different fabric, this is the extra yardage you will need, but don't reduce the Cap Fabric yardage.

Supplies

Light-weight paper-backed fusible web (for mittens, ski cap bands, and pom-pom bases): 1 yd.
HeatnBond® UltraHold Iron-on Adhesive (for Appli-bond pom-poms): 17" x ½ yd.
Embroidery floss (to match your mitten accent fabric colors, or black)

Templates

The circle, mitten, ski cap band, and 15° wedge templates for this project are on pages 35–38.
In place of the wedge template, you may use a Stack-n-Whack® 15° Fan Ruler (see Supplies and Resources on page 142).

 **Bundle Up**

Cutting the Cap Fabric

Prepare a 4-layer stack of the Cap Fabric, following the instructions on page 23.

Stack-n-Whack Chart for Bundle Up
Cut layers 21" wide. Cut 4 identical layers.

If the lengthwise design repeat is:	Use this many design repeats:		Make this many stacks:
Over 7"	1 repeat per layer		1

Whack...		To Make...
(1) 6" strip across the width		(9) 15° wedge block kits (See p. 28 for instructions on cutting 15° wedges)

Cutting Background, Border, and Binding Fabrics

Position in Quilt	First Cut	Second Cut
Triangles for under and between caps	(3) 9" strips across the width	(15) 9" 60° triangles* (6 per strip)
Half-triangles for row ends	(1) 9⅜" strip across the width	(3) 9⅜" 60° triangles.* Cut up the center on the straight of grain to make 6 half-triangles.
Sashing strips	(3) 2" strips across the width	Trim to fit quilt.
Background setting strips	(4) 6" strips across the width	
Border	(4) 3½" x 50" strips lengthwise. Cut the same portion of the stripe for each strip.	
Binding	(5) 2½" strips across the width	

*See p. 28 for instructions on cutting 60° triangles.

Piecing the Quilt Top

1. Use one block kit of identical wedges for each block. Sew the wedges together in pairs, right sides together, matching the top and bottom edges. Do not press the seam allowances yet.

2. Sew the pairs together, flipping the previous seam allowances away from the needle so that they will not get caught in the seam. To press the seam allowances open, start at the wide end and use just the tip of your iron.

3. Place each pieced wedge unit on a triangle, aligning the side edges. Baste close to the raw edges at the top and bottom (Fig. 2–1).

4. To make each row, sew the blocks, triangles, and half-triangles together. Measure the width across the center, and cut the three 2" sashing strips to this length. Sew a strip to the top of each pieced row (Fig. 2–2).

5. Sew the rows together as shown in the quilt assembly diagram (page 34). Measure the quilt from top to bottom through the center and cut two of the background fabric setting strips to this length. Sew these strips to two opposite sides. Measure across the width in the center of the quilt, including the setting strips, and cut the two remaining strips to this length. Sew them to the top and bottom.

Fusible Appliqué

1. To make templates, trace the patterns for the mitten (page 35), a reverse of the mitten, the ski cap band, and the 2" circle (page 38). Use the templates to trace the patterns on paper-backed fusible web, leaving an inch or so between each. Trace four left and four right mittens, nine bands, and nine 2" circles for the pom-pom bases. Cut the designs apart, leaving about ½" around the drawn lines.

2. Fuse the web to the wrong side of the accent fabrics, following the manufacturer's instructions. Make a pair of mittens of each color, three blue circles and bands, and two circles and bands from each of the other three colors. Cut along the traced lines.

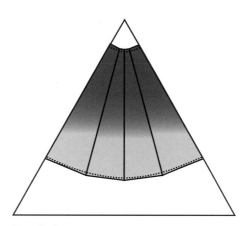

Fig. 2–1

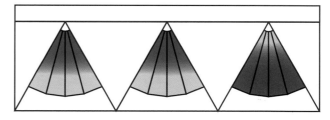

Fig. 2–2

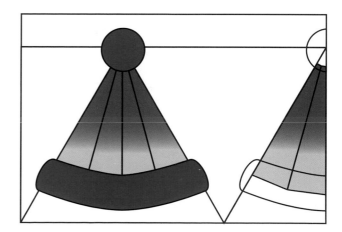

Fig. 2–3

3. Fuse the bands and 2" circles to the ski caps, placing them over the raw edges (Fig. 2–3, page 33).

4. Using the placement guide on pages 36–37, trace the lines for the strings and the tops of the mittens in each corner. Lay embroidery floss over the string lines and couch in place with a zigzag stitch. Position a pair of mittens in each corner, overlapping the ends of the floss. Fuse them in place.

5. Machine appliqué the circles, bands, and mittens with a blanket stitch, satin stitch, or other appliqué stitch.

Appli-bond Appliqué

1. From the blue fabric, cut two fabric pieces and one bonding piece 8½" x 9". Bond the pair of fabric pieces. Use the templates to trace three 3", three 2½", and three 2" circles on one side of the bonded blue fabric. Cut out the circles.

2. From the red, green, and purple fabrics, cut two fabric pieces and one bonding piece 6" x 8½". Bond each pair of fabric pieces. Use the templates to trace two 3", two 2½", and two 2" circles of each color from the bonded fabric. Cut out the circles.

3. Make cuts in each circle as shown by the straight lines in Figure 2–4, stopping about ¼" from the center of the circle.

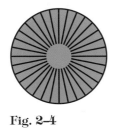

Fig. 2–4

4. Center a 3", a 2½" , and a 2" bonded circle on the 2" fused circle on the top of each ski cap.

Stitch in place by machine, making a small "x" in the center of the circles. To add dimension, heat with an iron and fluff the pom-poms with a quick brushing motion as shown in Plate 31 (page 19).

Adding Mitered Borders

Sew the strips to the sides of the quilt, mitering the corners.

Finishing

1. Cut the backing into two peices each 1½ yards long. Sew them together along the long edges.

2. Layer the quilt top, batting, and backing. Quilt the layers.

3. Join binding strips and bind the raw edges.

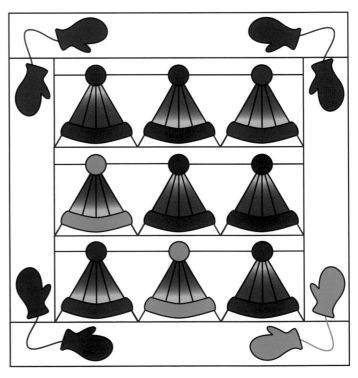

Quilt assembly

Mitten Placement

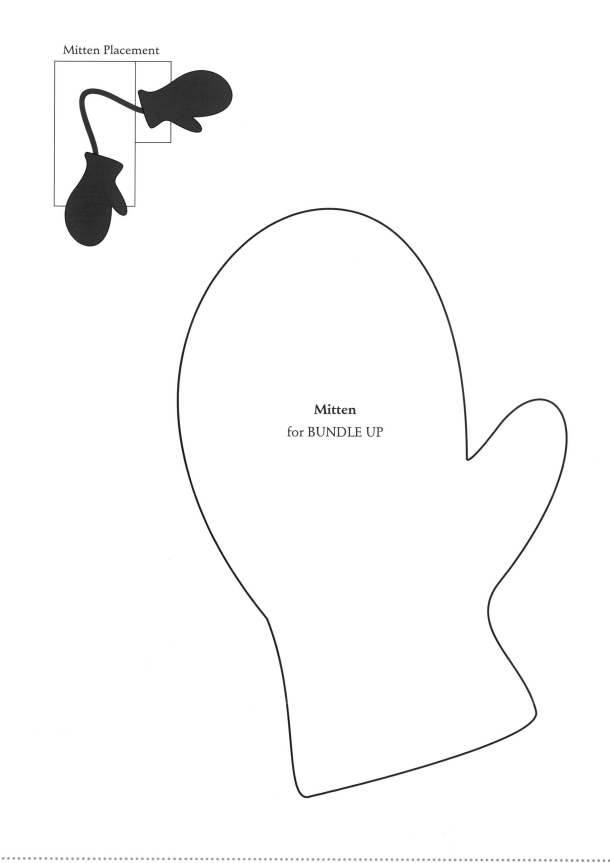

Mitten
for BUNDLE UP

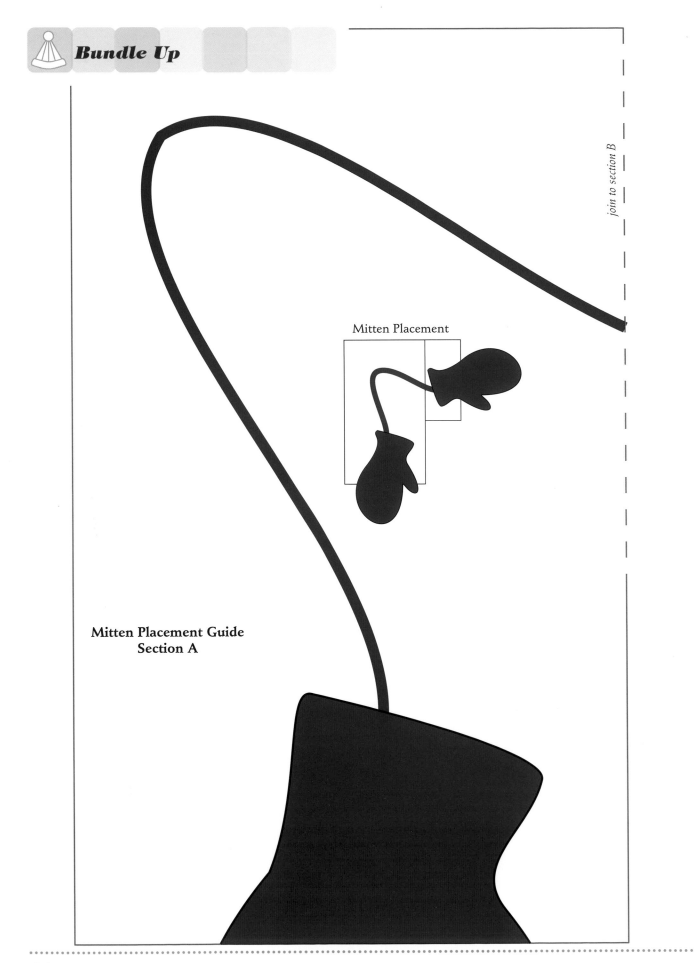

join to section B

Mitten Placement

**Mitten Placement Guide
Section A**

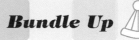
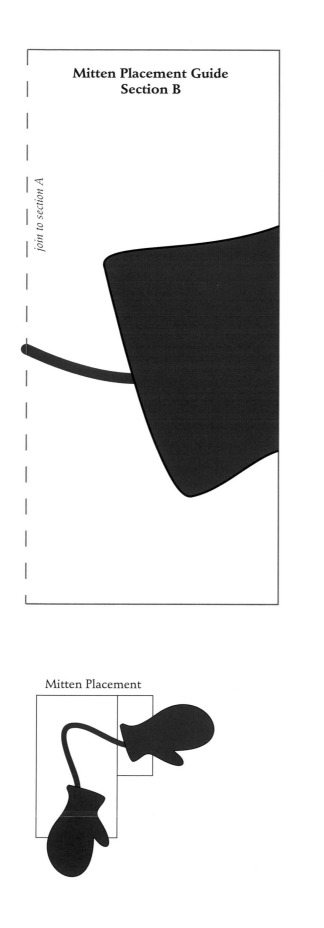

**Mitten Placement Guide
Section B**

join to section A

15° Wedge Template
for BUNDLE UP

Includes seam allowances

Mitten Placement

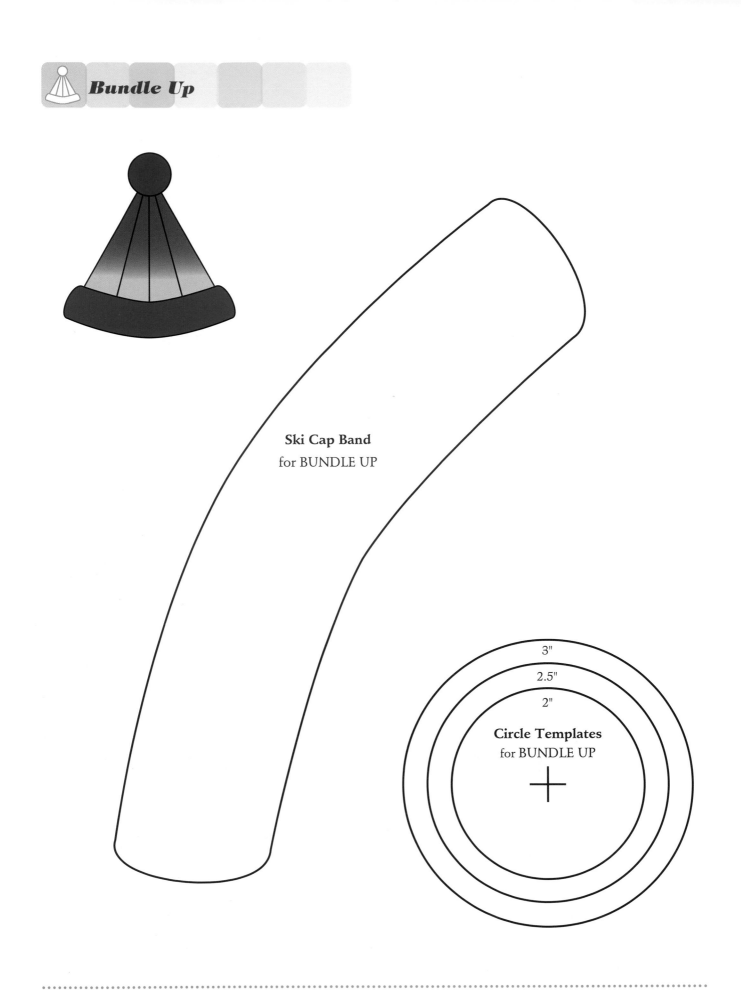

Ski Cap Band

for BUNDLE UP

3"

2.5"

2"

Circle Templates
for BUNDLE UP

February
Sweet Hearts Wall Quilt

Designed by Karen Combs and Bethany Reynolds. Machined pieced by Karen Combs. Machine quilted by Judy Irish. Karen's original heart design has the illusion of depth. For the wall quilt, she asked Bethany to add a Stack-n-Whack twist to the heart, so Bethany used the Magic Mirror-Image Trick to create a very special design. For the table runner, page 45, Karen selected three heart colors and used a darker value for the side of each heart to enhance the illusion of depth. The hearts look so real that it's hard to believe they are actually flat!

Sweet Hearts Wall Quilt

Skill level: **Average**

Finished block: **7" x 6"**

Finished quilt: **43" x 40"**

Before beginning, review the fabric selection tips for Karen's Quilts of Illusion (page 13). For the wall quilt, also review Bethany's fabric selection tips for the Stack-n-Whack Magic Mirror-Image Trick (pages 15–16) and the general instructions for Stack-n-Whack (page 21).

Directions for the table runner begin on page 45.

Fabric Requirements

Measurements are in yards unless otherwise indicated.

If the design repeat of the **Heart Fabric** (piece A) is:	7"–10"	11"–14"	15"–17"	18"–26"	over 26"
You will need this many yards for the Stack-n-Whack blocks:	⅞	1⅛	1¼	1¾	2 repeats

Additional Fabrics	
Light – background	⅝
Dark Red – heart sides	⅜
Red – side window frames	¼
Medium Pink – bottom window frames	¼
Dark blue – sashing	⅝
Border	½
Backing (pieced crosswise)	2½
Binding	⅜

Cutting the Heart Fabric

Prepare a two-layer stack of the heart fabric, following the instructions on page 21.

Stack-n-Whack Chart for Sweet Hearts (front of hearts, piece A)		
Cut layers 21" wide. Cut 2 identical layers.		
If the lengthwise design repeat is:	**Use this many design repeats:**	**Make this many stacks:**
6" – 14"	1 repeat per layer	2
over 14"	1 repeat per layer	1
Whack...	**To Make...**	
(2) 6½" strips across the width	(9) 3½" by 6½" rectangle block kits	

Cutting Background and Accent Fabrics chart on page 42

Making the Blocks

Make 9 heart blocks as follows:

1. To make triangle units, cut the 2¼" squares (B) of light background and dark red heart side fabrics twice on the diagonal to make 4 triangles. Piece as shown in Figure 2–5, with the light background fabric on the left. Use a ruler to trim the tips 1½" from the right-angle corner (Plate 45).

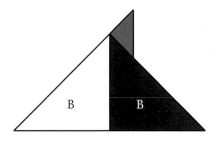

Fig. 2–5

2. For the Stack-n-Whack Magic Mirror-Image Trick, you will use one block kit of 2 identical rectangles of the main fabric for each heart. To create each heart's symmetrical design, the reverse side of the fabric will be face up on one half of the heart.

Lay out 2 rectangles so that the fabric on the left side faces right side up and the fabric on the right side is the reverse. This will form a mirror image at the center. Place a pin in the center edge of both pieces to remind you that each heart uses a right and a reverse side of the fabric (Plate 46, page 43).

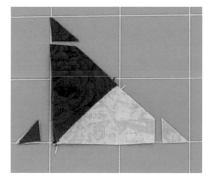

Plate 45. Trim the tips 1½" from the right-angle corner.

Cutting Background and Accent Fabrics

Position in Quilt	First Cut	Second Cut
Light – Background	(2) 3½" strips across the width	(9) 3½" squares (D) and (9) 1½" x 3½" rectangles (F)
Light – Background	(1) 2½" strip across the width	(9) 2½" squares (E)
Light – Background	(1) 1½" x 30" strip	(18) 1½" squares (C)
Light – Background	(1) 2¼" x 10" strip	(3) 2¼" squares (B)
Light – Background	(7) 1¼" strips across the width	(18) 1¼" x 6½" (G) strips and (18) 1¼" x 9" strips (H)
Dark red – heart sides	(2) 3½" strips across the width	(9) 3½" squares (D) and (9) 1½" x 3½" rectangles (F)
Dark red – heart sides	(1) 1½" strip across the width	(27) 1½" squares (C)
Dark red – heart sides	(1) 2¼" x 10" strip	(3) 2¼" squares (B)
Red – side window frames	(3) 2¼" strips across the width	(9) 2¼" x 8" strips (I)
Red – side window frames	(1) 2⅝" x 18" strip	(5) 2⅝" squares. Cut each square once on the diagonal to make (10) half-square triangles (J).
Medium pink – bottom window frames	(3) 2¼" strips across the width	(9) 2¼" x 9" strips (K)
Medium pink – bottom window frames	(1) 2⅝" x 18" strip	(5) 2⅝" squares. Cut each square once on the diagonal to make (10) half-square triangles (J).
Dark blue – sashing	(8) 2" strips across the width	See Adding Sashing and Borders (page 44) for cutting instructions
Dark red – outer border	(4) 3½" strips across the width	
Binding	(5) 2½" strips across the width	

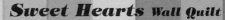

3. For the left side of the heart, sew a 1½" dark red square (C), a B/B triangle unit, and a 3½" dark red heart side square (D) on the main fabric (left side of Plate 47). For the right side of the heart, sew a 1½" dark red heart side square (C), a 1½" light background square (C), and a 3½" light background square (D) on the main fabric (right side of Plate 47). Trim the seam allowances to ¼" and press them away from the main fabric.

4. On left side of the heart, sew a 2½" light background (E) square (Fig. 2–6). Trim the seam allowances to ¼" and press them toward the red fabric.

5. To complete the left side of the hearts, sew a 1½" light background square (C) on a 1½" x 3½" dark red heart side rectangle (F) and a 1½" dark red heart square on a 1½" x 3½" light background (F) rectangle (Fig. 2–7).

Trim the seam allowances to ¼" and press them toward the red fabric. Sew the units together (Fig. 2–8).

6. Sew 1¼" x 6½" light background pieces (G) to the right and left sides. Sew 1¼" x 9" light

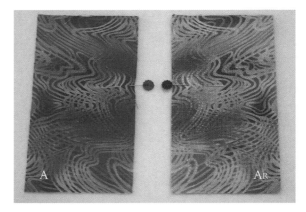

Plate 46. Place a pin in the center edges of both pieces of a block kit.

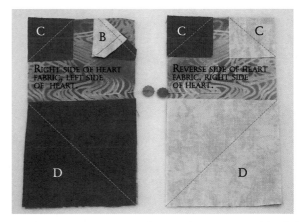

Plate 47. Sew squares and triangle units to a block kit to make the two halves of a heart.

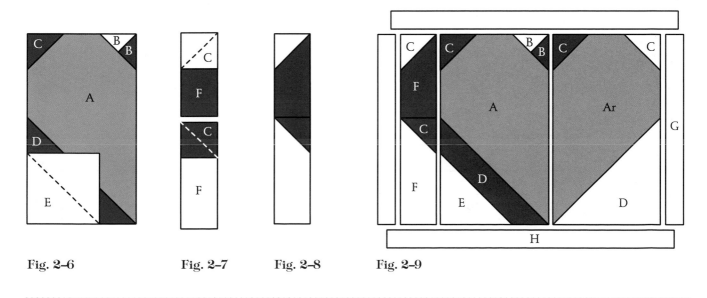

Fig. 2–6   Fig. 2–7   Fig. 2–8   Fig. 2–9

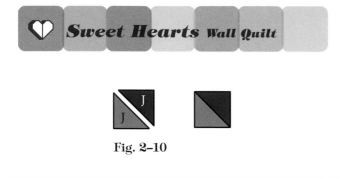

Fig. 2–10

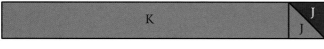

Fig. 2–11

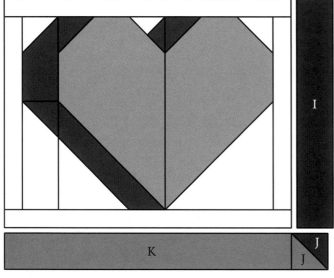

Fig. 2–12

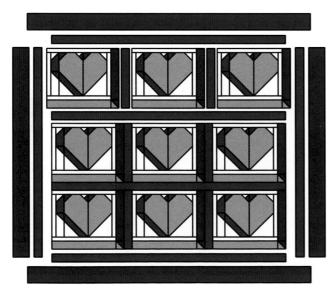

Quilt assembly

background pieces (H) to the top and bottom (Fig. 2–9, page 43).

Assembling the Quilt

1. To make window frames, join the bottom window frame triangles (Fig. 2–10). Sew a triangle unit to a bottom window frame rectangle (Fig. 2–11).

2. Sew a side window frame rectangle (I) to the heart block. Add the unit you made in Step 1 to the bottom of the block (Fig. 2–12).

Adding Sashing and Borders

1. To add the dark blue sashing, first join the dark blue 2" x 9½" sashing rectangles and the heart blocks to make each row (see the quilt assembly diagram on this page). Measure the width across the center of one row. Cut four 2" dark blue sashing strips to that length. Use these strips to sew the rows together at the top and bottom. To complete, measure down the center, including the sashing strips, and cut two 2" dark blue strips that length. Sew them to the right and left sides.

2. Measure the quilt top down the center and cut two 3½" border strips to this length. Sew the borders to the right and left sides.

3. Measure across the width in the center of the quilt, including the borders, and cut two 3½" borders this measurement. Sew them to the top and bottom.

Finishing

1. Prepare the backing by piecing together two 1¼-yard lengths of backing fabric.

2. Layer the quilt top, batting, and backing. Quilt the layers.

3. Join the 2½" strips and bind the raw edges.

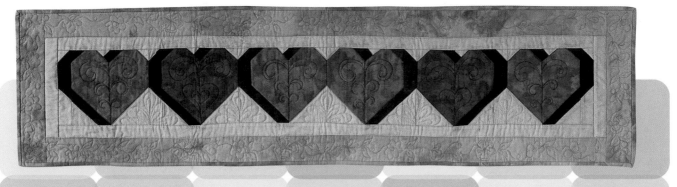

February
Sweet Hearts Table Runner

Skill level: Average

Finished block: **7" x 6"**

Finished quilt: **14" x 50"**

Designed & machine pieced by Karen Combs.
Machine quilted by Judy Irish.

Cutting Fabrics

Position in Quilt	First Cut	Second Cut
Cream – Background	(1) 3½" strip across the width	(6) 3½" squares (D) and (6) 1½" x 3½" rectangles (F)
Cream – Background	(1) 2½ x 18" strip	(6) 2½" squares (E)
Cream – Background	(1) 1½" x 20" strip	(12) 1½" squares (C)
Cream – Background	(1) 2¼" x 8" strip	(3) 2¼" squares (B)
Cream – Inner border	(3) 1½" strips across the width	See Assembling the Quilt page 46
Light blue – outer border	(3) 3½" strips across the width	See Assembling the Quilt page 46
Medium – front of hearts	(1) 3½" strip across the width per color	(4) 3½" x 6½" rectangles of each color (A)
Dark – sides of hearts	(1) 3½" x 12" strip	(2) 3½" squares (D) of each color and (2) 1½" x 3½" rectangles (F) of each color
Dark – sides of hearts	(1) 1½" x 10" strip	(6) 1½" squares (C) of each color
Dark – sides of hearts	(1) 2¼" square (B) of each color	
Binding	(4) 2½" strips across the width	

Making the Blocks

Make 6 heart blocks as follows:

1. Follow Steps 1 (page 41) and 3 through 5 (page 43) to make 3 hearts, one in each of the medium and dark color combinations.

2. Make 3 reversed heart blocks, one in each color combination (Fig. 2–13). Note that the B triangles are reversed.

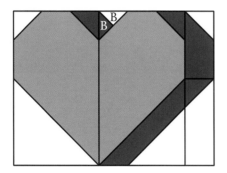

Fig. 2–13

Assembling the Quilt

Following the quilt assembly diagram, sew the hearts together. Measure across the width in the center of the table runner, and cut two 1½" inner cream border strips this length. If your fabric is less than 43" wide, cut and sew the extra length as needed. Sew the strips to the top and bottom. Measure down in the center of the table runner and cut two 1½" cream inner border strips this length. Sew them to the sides. Likewise, measure, cut, and sew the 3½" light blue outer border strips to the table runner.

Finishing

1. Prepare the backing by cutting the fabric piece in half down its length. Sew the two panels together on the short sides.

2. Layer the quilt top, batting, and backing. Quilt the layers

3. Join the 2½" strips and bind the raw edges.

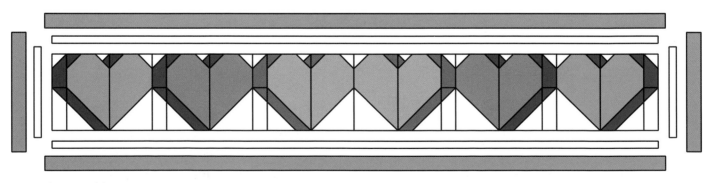

Quilt assembly

March
Rockin' Robin

Designed and appliquéd by Joan Shay. Machine quilted by Judy Irish. These are Joan's first quilts using Appli-bond to make birds. It is very easy and effective. The dimension in the feathers is very realistic. You can almost smell the apple blossoms!

Skill level: **Average**

Finished quilt: 33" x 25"

Rockin' Robin

Before beginning, review the instructions for Appli-bond on page 17.
Directions for LAST ONE OUT begin on page 54.

Fabric Requirements

Measurements are in yards unless otherwise indicated.

Fabric	ROCKIN' ROBIN	LAST ONE OUT
Background	⅝	⅜
Blossom – light pink (pieces 9 & 10)	¼	
Blossom – dark pink (pieces 9 & 10)	⅛	
Leaves (piece 8)	⅛ each of 2 shades	
Leaves – green (piece 15)		3" x 7" scrap
Tree limb – medium brown ROCKIN' ROBIN (piece 1) LAST ONE OUT (piece 11)	½	8" x 11" scrap
Robin – foundation, head (piece 6), and body feathers (pieces 4 & 5) – medium brown ROCKIN' ROBIN and LAST ONE OUT (piece 13)	⅜	4" x 5" scrap
Feathers – medium-dark brown (piece 12)		4" x 5" scrap
Tail feathers – light brown (piece 2)	1" x 8" scrap	
Body accent feathers – dark brown (piece 3)	1" x 8" scrap	
Robin's breast – red (piece 4)	⅛	
Throat feathers – light tan (piece 3)	1" x 1½" scrap	
Nest – tan and brown		9" long scraps of each color
Beak – orange (piece 7)	1½" x 1½" scrap	
Beak – yellow (piece 14)		1½" x 1½" scrap
Backing	⅞	⅝
Borders and binding	⅞	⅜

Supplies

HeatnBond® UltraHold Iron-on Adhesive: 1 yd. for ROCKIN' ROBIN
¼ yd. for LAST ONE OUT

Appli-bond needle

ROCKIN' ROBIN:
Nylon beading thread: green (size D)
Glass seed beads: yellow (size 10)
Embroidery floss: green to match leaves
Pebble bead (2.5 mm in size) for robin's eye

LAST ONE OUT:
Nylon beading thread: Black (size D)
Embroidery floss: brown, yellow, and green
Water-soluble stabilizer such as Solvy®: 2 pieces 7" x 9"
Button (¼" in size) for the bird's eye

Templates

ROCKIN' ROBIN templates for tree limb, small and large blossoms, leaf, robin foundation, head, beak, and feathers are on pages 51–53.

LAST ONE OUT templates for the tree limb, leaf, nest shape, robin foundation, head, beak, and feather are on page 57.

ROCKIN' ROBIN
Appli-bond Appliqué

1. Cut the following:
❧ Light blossoms: two fabric pieces and one bonding piece 8" x 17"
❧ Dark blossoms: two fabric pieces and one bonding piece 2" x 17"
❧ Leaves: two fabric pieces from each color and two bonding pieces 2" x 17"
❧ Red breast: two fabric pieces and one bonding piece 4" x 8"

❧ Light tan throat: two fabric pieces and one bonding piece 1" x 1½"
❧ Light brown tail feathers: two fabric pieces and one bonding piece 1" x 8"
❧ Medium brown robin foundation, head, and body feathers: two fabric pieces and one bonding piece 12" x 15"
❧ Dark brown body accent feathers: 2 pieces of fabric and one bonding piece 1" x 8"
❧ Orange beak: two pieces 1½" x 1½"

2. Bond pair of fabrics together. Prepare templates for the robin foundation (page 53), feathers (pieces 2, 3, 4, and 5), head (piece 6), beak (piece 7), leaf (piece 8), and blossoms (pieces 9 and 10) on pages 51–53. Trace the number of pieces from each fabric as indicated on the template pieces. Cut out on the line. (A seam allowance is not needed for Appli-bond).

Traditional Appliqué

1. Cut the background fabric 17½" x 25½".

2. Use a photocopy machine to increase the tree limb (piece 1) by 200 percent. Make a template from the tree limb pattern. Trace the template on the limb fabric and cut it, adding a ³⁄₁₆" turn-under allowance by eye.

3. Appliqué the limb on the background. The base of the limb should be 6¼" up from the bottom edge on the right side of the quilt.

Attaching Appli-bond Pieces

The robin is constructed on its bonded foundation piece before it is attached to the background. In Steps 1–5 that follow, use the robin foundation pattern (page 53) to trace onto your template all lines within the robin's body. This will help you to place the Appli-bond pieces in their correct positions. For the stab stitches and seed beads, see the pattern pieces (pages 51–53) for placement.

1. Use an Appli-bond needle for the feathers, because you will be going through several thicknesses. Work from the tail end and overlap them slightly as you progress toward the head. Transfer the placement lines to the bonded foundation. Follow the shape of the foundation for the outside pieces. Using two stab stitches for each feather, attach them in the following order: light brown tail, dark brown accent on wings, red breast, dark brown accent on breast, medium brown body, and medium brown wing (Fig. 2–14).

2. Place the head (piece 6) so that it overlaps the top of the feathers. Attach it and then the two throat feathers (light tan piece 3) to the foundation with French knots (page 20). Use two strands of embroidery floss and wrap the Appli-bond needle three times.

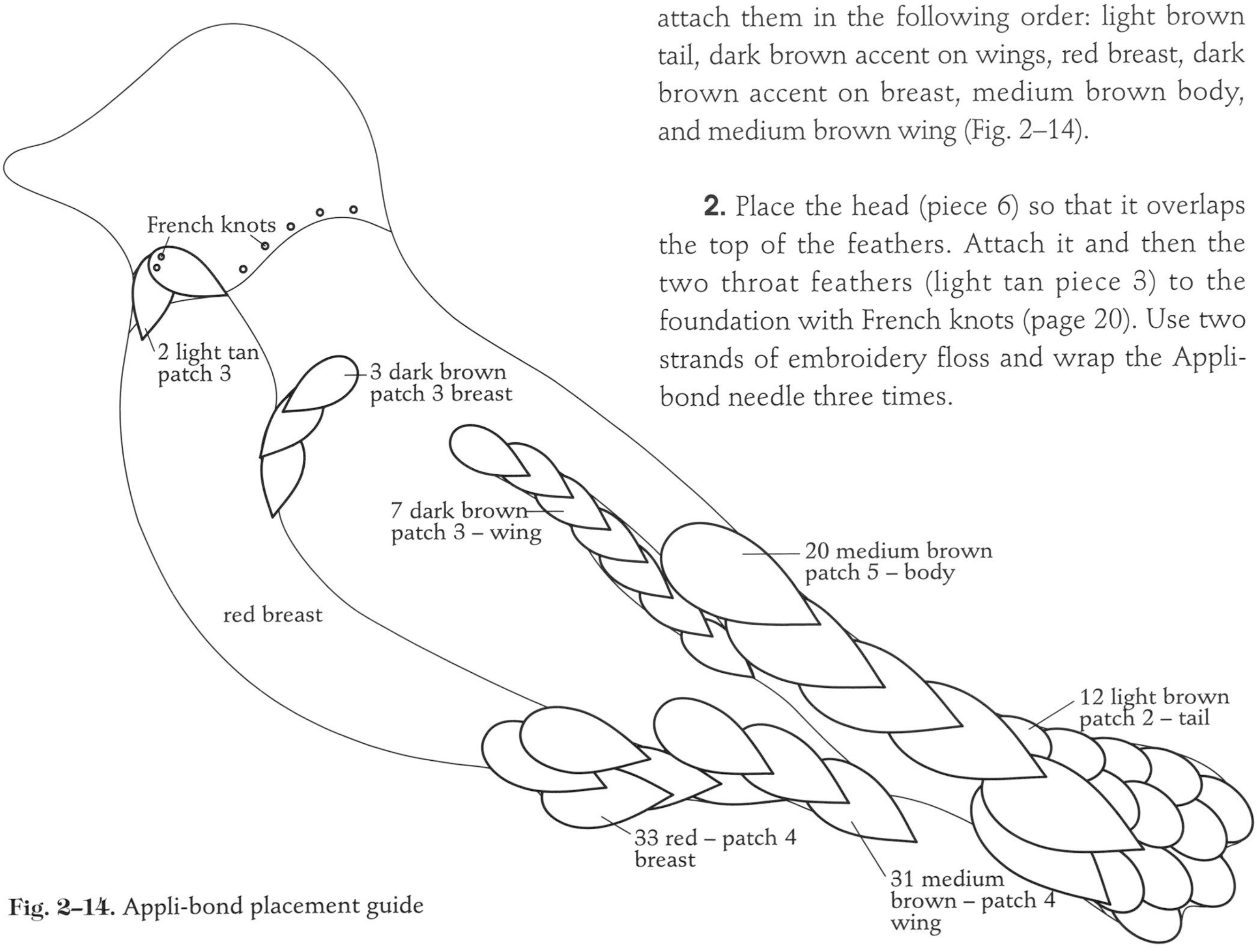

Fig. 2–14. Appli-bond placement guide

3. Attach the beak (piece 7) with a stem stitch (page 20), using two strands of embroidery floss.

4. Trim any foundation that shows beyond the feathers. You now have a completed robin.

5. Pin the robin in position on the tree limb, but don't attach him yet. Scatter leaves on the tree limb, placing a few leaves (piece 8) under the robin so, when the blossoms are added, the robin's "feet" are not visible. Removing the robin for now, attach the leaves to the background with stem stitches (page 20) as indicated on the pattern (page 52). Use two strands of embroidery floss and an Appli-bond needle.

6. Using green nylon bead thread, attach the blossoms (pieces 9 and 10) by sewing four yellow seed beads in the center of each blossom.

7. Position the robin so his "feet" are hidden by the blossoms. Lift the feathers and attach the foundation of the robin to the background with stab stitches placed about an inch apart.

8. Secure the head by sewing the 2.5 mm robin's eye bead with nylon beading thread through the background.

9. Curl the leaves by heating with an iron and folding over your finger. Hold the shape until cool. To curl the blossoms, heat with an iron and rub your hand over them in a back and forth motion as shown on Plate 31 (page 19).

Adding Butted Borders

1. Cut three 4½" wide strips across the width of the border fabric.

2. Measure the quilt top down the center and cut two borders this length. Sew the borders to two opposite sides.

3. Measure across the width in the center of the quilt, including borders, and cut two borders this length. Sew them to the top and bottom.

Finishing

1. Layer the quilt top, batting, and backing.

2. Quilt the layers.

3. Cut four 2½" strips across the width of the binding fabric. Join the binding strips and bind the raw edges.

Full-sized Feather Patterns

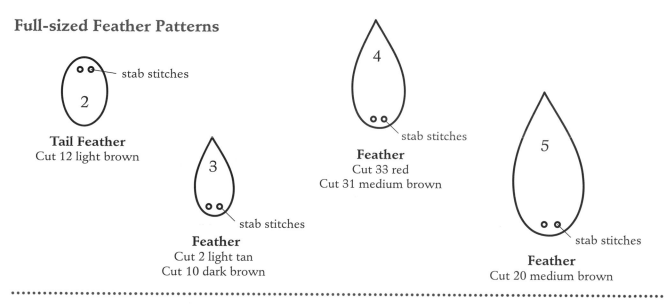

stab stitches

2

Tail Feather
Cut 12 light brown

3

stab stitches

Feather
Cut 2 light tan
Cut 10 dark brown

4

stab stitches

Feather
Cut 33 red
Cut 31 medium brown

5

stab stitches

Feather
Cut 20 medium brown

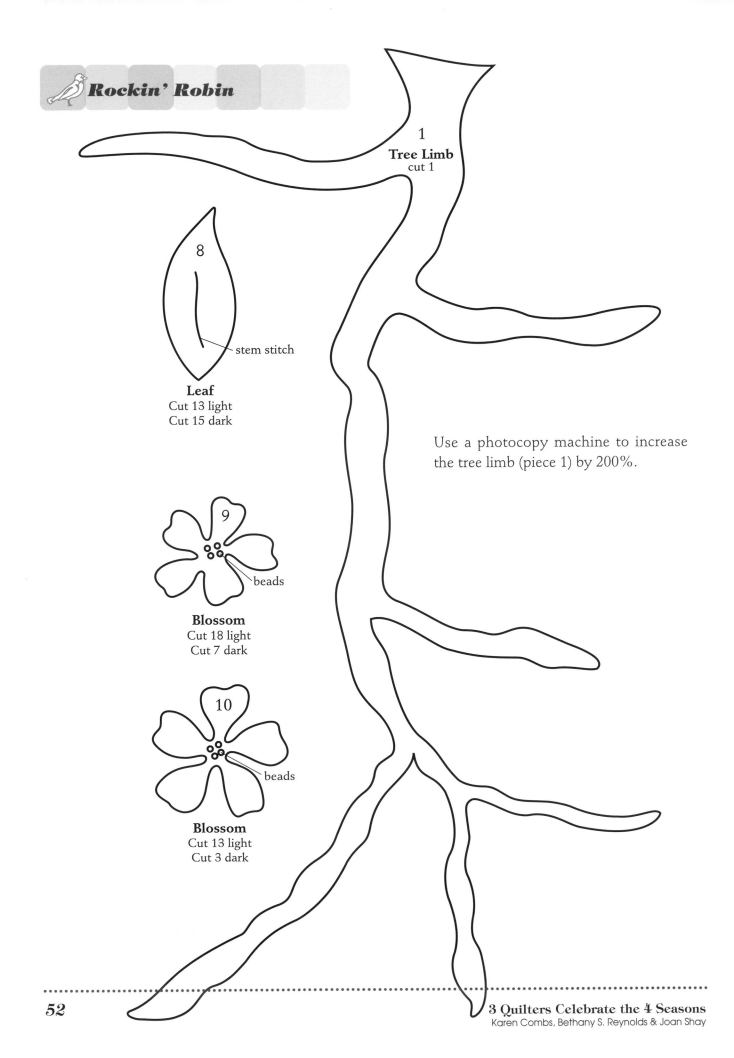

Tree Limb
cut 1

1

8

stem stitch

Leaf
Cut 13 light
Cut 15 dark

Use a photocopy machine to increase the tree limb (piece 1) by 200%.

9

beads

Blossom
Cut 18 light
Cut 7 dark

10

beads

Blossom
Cut 13 light
Cut 3 dark

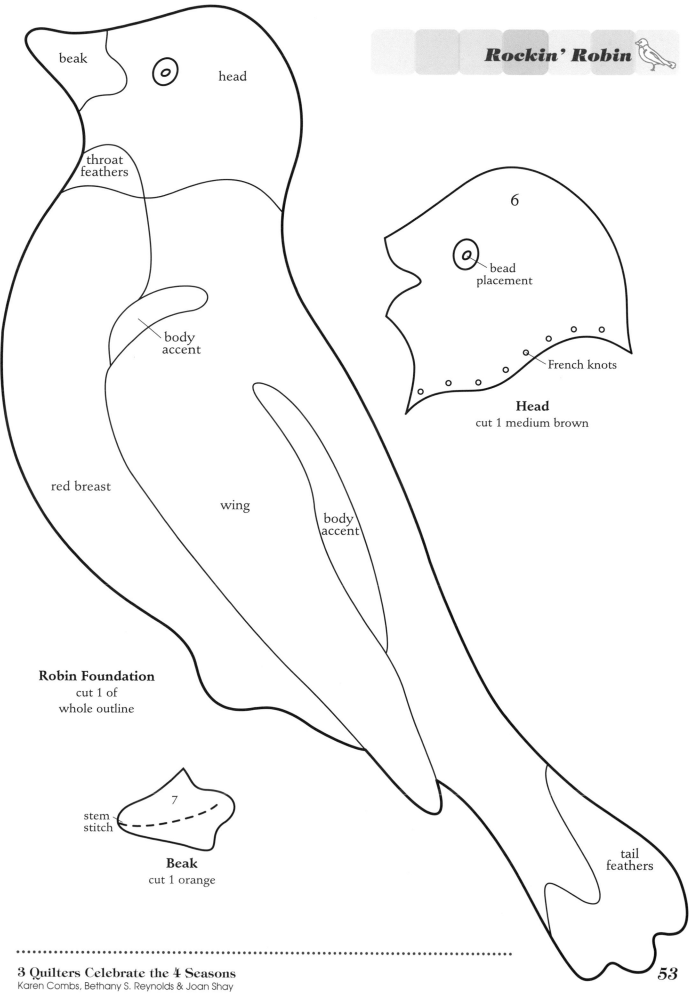

beak

head

Rockin' Robin

throat
feathers

6

bead
placement

French knots

Head
cut 1 medium brown

body
accent

red breast

wing

body
accent

Robin Foundation
cut 1 of
whole outline

stem
stitch

7

Beak
cut 1 orange

tail
feathers

March
Last One Out

Designed, appliquéd, and machine quilted by Joan Shay. Nest by Bethany Reynolds. These are Joan's first quilts using Appli-bond to make birds. It is very easy and effective. The dimension in the feathers is very realistic. You can see by the chunky size of the baby robin that he is the last to leave the nest.

Before beginning, review the instructions for Appli-bond on page 17.
Refer to the Fabric Requirements chart on page 48.

LAST ONE OUT
Appli-bond Appliqué

1. Cut the following:
   ❧ Medium brown foundation and head: Cut 2 fabric pieces and 1 bonding piece 4" x 5"
   ❧ Medium-dark brown feathers: Cut 2 fabric pieces and 1 bonding piece 4" x 5"
   ❧ Yellow beak: Cut 2 fabric pieces and 1 bonding piece 1½" x 1½"
   ❧ Green leaves: Cut 2 fabric pieces and 1 bonding piece 3" x 7"

2. Bond the fabric pieces together. Prepare templates for the robin foundation and the feathers, head, beak, and leaves. Trace the number of pieces from each fabric as indicated on the template pieces (page 57). Cut on the line (a seam allowance is not needed for Appli-bond).

Plate 48. Arrange narrow strips on the stabilizer, extending them slightly beyond the nest outline. Place the second piece of stabilizer on top and pin around the edges.

Building the Bird's Nest

1. Use a permanent marker to trace the nest shape (page 57) on one piece of the water-soluble stabilizer.

2. From the tan and brown scraps, cut a generous handful of strips about 9" long and ⅛" to ⅜" wide. Arrange the strips on the marked stabilizer, extending them slightly beyond the outline of the nest. Place the second piece of stabilizer on top and pin around the edges (Plate 48).

3. Using a blending thread color, stitch back and forth across the nest shape to secure the fabric strips (Plate 49).

4. Soak the nest in water to dissolve the stabilizer, rinse, and let dry.

Plate 49. Use a thread color that blends with the strips and stitch across the nest to secure the fabric strips.

Traditional Appliqué

1. Cut the background fabric into one piece 10½" x 12½".

2. Make a template for the tree limb (piece 11) and trace onto the medium-brown fabric. Cut out, adding a ³⁄₁₆" turn-under allowance by eye.

3. Place the base of the tree limb on the right side of the quilt about 1¾" up from the bottom edge of the background. Appliqué the tree limb to the background fabric.

Attaching the Appli-bond Pieces

The baby robin is constructed on its bonded foundation piece before it is attached to the background. For the French knots (page 20), stab stitches (page 20), and stem stitches (page 20) in the steps below, see the patterns (page 57) for placement. Use an Appli-bond needle for these stitches.

1. Referring to the Appli-bond placement guide (Fig. 2–15), attach the feathers (piece 12) to the foundation with two stab stitches. Work from the bottom and overlap slightly as you progress toward the head.

2. Attach the head (piece 13) with French knots, using 2 strands of embroidery floss and wrapping the needle 3 times.

3. Attach the beak (piece 14) to the head with two French knots. Heat the bonded beak with an iron and gently fold along the fold line.

4. Pin the nest in place on the tree limb. Pin the bird in place, so that it is sitting in the nest. Lift the feathers and attach the bird to the background with two stab stitches. Using thread to match, attach the nest to the background with stab stitches.

5. Secure the head by sewing the button with nylon beading thread through the background.

6. Scatter the leaves (piece 15) on the tree limb and attach them to the background with the stem stitches (page 20) as indicated on the pattern (page 57). Use 2 strands of embroidery floss. Curl each leaf by heating with an iron and shaping it over your finger. Hold the shape until cool (Plate 29, page 18).

Adding Butted Borders

1. Cut 4 strips 2½" across the width of the border and binding fabric.

2. Measure the quilt top down the center and cut two borders this length. Sew the borders to two opposite sides.

3. Measure across the width in the center of the quilt, including borders, and cut two borders this length. Sew them to the top and bottom. Set aside remaining strips for the binding.

Finishing

1. Layer the quilt top, batting, and backing.

2. Quilt the layers.

3. Use the remaining 2½" border strips for the binding. Join the strips and bind the raw edges.

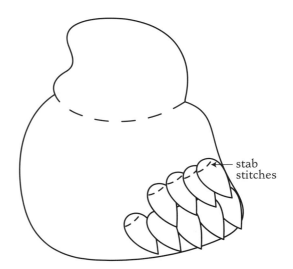

Fig. 2–15. Appli-bond placement guide

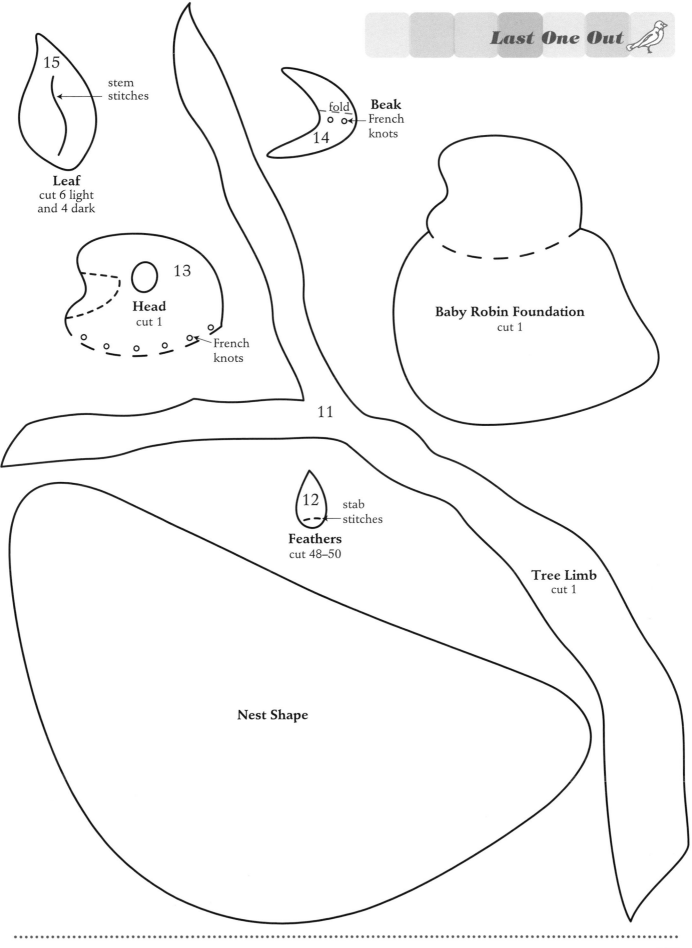

15
stem
stitches
Leaf
cut 6 light
and 4 dark

fold
Beak
French
knots
14

13
Head
cut 1
French
knots

Baby Robin Foundation
cut 1

11

12
stab
stitches
Feathers
cut 48–50

Tree Limb
cut 1

Nest Shape

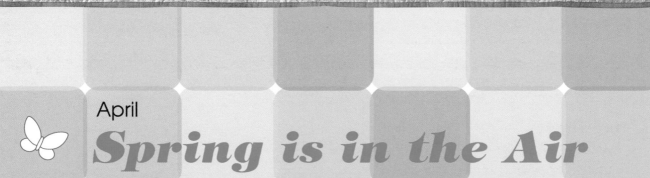

April

Spring is in the Air

Designed and appliquéd by Joan Shay with pieced background by Bethany Reynolds. Machine quilted by Judy Irish. Joan's wheelbarrow filled with sweet pea flowers captures the promise of spring. Joan asked Bethany to design a pieced background to complement the appliqué. The butterfly just happened by.

Before beginning, review the instructions for Appli-bond on page 17.

Fabric Requirements
Measurements are in yards unless otherwise indicated.

Background fabric A – light wedges, triangles, and squares	1⅛
Background fabric B – medium wedges and triangles	⅞
Background fabric C – border wedges and triangles	⅝
Wheelbarrow	¼
Flowers	⅛ each of 6
Leaves	¼
Other appliqué fabrics	scraps for wheel, inner wheel, stand, and handle (pieces 5–7 & 9) and butterfly novelty print
Backing	1½
Binding (cut [4] 2½" strips crosswise)	½

Supplies

HeatnBond® UltraHold Iron-on Adhesive: 1½ yds.
Glass beads: 48 green in size 6
Nylon bead thread: green (size D)
Embroidery floss: green
Appli-bond needle
Embroidery needle

Templates

Templates for pieces 1–9 are on pages 64–65. A template for the 45-degree triangle wedge is on page 63. A template for the flower and leaf placement is on pages 66–67.

Cutting Background Fabrics

Position in Quilt	First Cut	Second Cut
Background fabric A – light wedges	(5) 4" strips across the width	(100) 45° triangles wedges*
Background fabric A – light corner triangles	(1) 2⅝" strip across the width	(8) 2⅝" squares. Cut each square once on the diagonal to make (16) half-square triangles
Background fabric A – light squares	(2) 6½" strips across the width	(8) 6½" squares
Background fabric B – medium wedges	(4) 4" strips across the width	(68) 45° triangle wedges*
Background fabric B – medium corner triangles	(3) 2⅝" strips across the width	(34) 2⅝" squares. Cut each square once on the diagonal to make (68) half-square triangles
Background fabric C – border wedges	(3) 4" strips across the width	(48) 45° triangle wedges*
Background fabric C – border corner triangles	(1) 2⅝" strip across the width	(12) 2⅝" squares. Cut each square once on the diagonal to make (24) half-square triangles
Binding	(4) 2½" strips across the width	

*See p. 26 for instructions on cutting 45° triangle wedges.

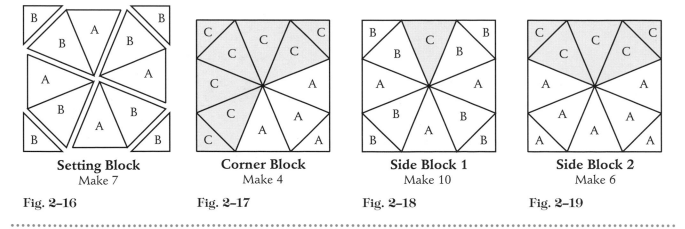

Setting Block
Make 7

Fig. 2–16

Corner Block
Make 4

Fig. 2–17

Side Block 1
Make 10

Fig. 2–18

Side Block 2
Make 6

Fig. 2–19

3 Quilters Celebrate the 4 Seasons
Karen Combs, Bethany S. Reynolds & Joan Shay

Making the Background

1. To make the blocks, follow the diagrams (Figs. 2–16 through 2–19, page 60) to place the correct A, B, and C background fabrics in each block.

Piece each block in the following order. After each seam, press the allowances open unless indicated otherwise:

❖ Sew 4 pairs of triangle wedges together from the outer edge in.

❖ To make 2 halves, sew 2 pairs together from the outer edge in. Repeat with the other 2 pairs. Clip the triangle tips.

❖ Pin the 2 halves together, carefully matching the seams in the center. Stitch, press, and then clip the triangle tips.

❖ Add corner triangles to the 4 sides, centering them on the wedges. Press the seam allowances toward the triangles. Clip the triangle tips.

2. Join the blocks and the 6½" squares of fabric A in rows as shown in the quilt assembly diagram on page 63. Join the rows.

Appli-bond Appliqué

1. Cut 2 fabric pieces from each of the 6 flower fabrics and cut 6 pieces of Heat-n-Bond each 4½" x 17". Cut 2 pieces of the leaf fabric and a piece of Heat-n-Bond each 8" x 17".

2. Joining pairs of the same color, bond the flower fabrics together. Bond the 2 pieces of leaf fabrics.

3. Make templates (pages 64–65) for pieces 1–4. On one side of each bonded flower fabric, use the templates to trace eight each of pieces 1 and 2. On one side of the flower leaf fabric, trace 48 of piece 3 and 24 of piece 4. Cut out the pieces on the lines (no seam allowances are needed for Appli-bond).

4. Make a small cut in each piece 1 as indicated on the template (page 64.). Curl the piece by heating with an iron and folding the top section down where indicated (Plate 50). Then shape the top section around your index finger (Plate 51). Hold the shape between your thumb and middle finger until cool.

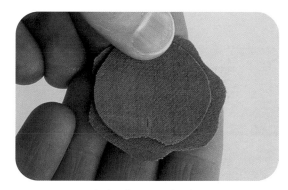

Plate 50. Curl the flowers by heating with an iron and folding the top section down.

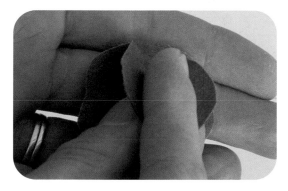

Plate 51. Shape the top section up around your index finger.

Plate 52. Heat, fold in half lengthwise, and hold until cool.

5. Heat a piece 2. Fold in half lengthwise without creasing the fold. Hold the shape until cool (Plate 52, page 61).

6. The flowers are assembled before attaching them to the background. To make each flower, layer a piece 1, 2, and then 3. Use an Appli-bond needle to secure the pieces with a stab stitch (page 20) where indicated in Figure 2–20.

7. Cut two butterfly images a little larger than the print. Cut a piece of the adhesive the same size. Bond the images wrong sides together. Cut out the butterfly image.

Traditional Appliqué

1. Trace the templates for the wheels, stand, wheelbarrow, and handle (pieces 5–9) on pages 64–65. Join the two pieces for pieces 8 and 9. Make templates for the pieces. Trace one of each on the appropriate fabrics and cut them out, adding a ³⁄₁₆" turn-under allowance by eye.

2. Place the bottom of the larger wheel 6" from the bottom of the pieced background and 13" from the left edge. Appliqué the pieces to the background in numerical order.

Attaching Appli-bond Pieces

1. Trace the flower and leaf placement templates (pages 66–67). Join them, and then cut out along the outer lines. Align the wheelbarrow placement lines with the appliquéd wheelbarrow. Trace around the template with a blue water-soluble pen (the flowers lift off the background, so it is necessary to use an erasable marking tool).

2. Place the Appli-bonded leaves in position as marked on the background. Scatter the remaining leaves as shown in the quilt photograph. Using a stem stitch (page 20) and 2 strands of green embroidery floss threaded on an Appli-bond needle, sew each in place along the vein line (see leaf template on page 65).

3. Curl the bonded leaves by heating with an iron and folding over your finger. Hold the shape until cool (Plate 29, page 18).

4. Scatter the flowers over the background, using the traced blue line as a guide for the outer edges. Using nylon bead thread and an Appli-bond needle, attach the flowers to the background by sewing a bead over the stab stitch. Tie off the thread of each bead securely on the back.

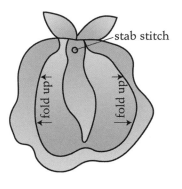

Fig. 2–20

Fig. 2–21

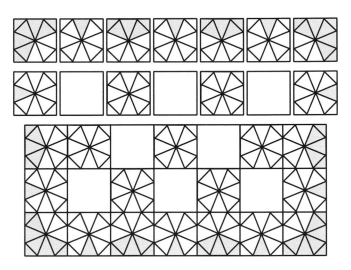

5. Thread your embroidery needle with one strand of embroidery floss. Stem stitch tendrils (Fig. 2–21) around the edges of the flowers, scattering them as you wish.

6. Attach the Appli-bonded butterfly with 3 French knots (page 20) along the body of the butterfly. Use 2 strands of embroidery floss and wrap the Appli-bond needle 3 times. Heat the bonded butterfly and bend the wings into a pleasing shape. Hold until the piece is cool.

Finishing

1. Layer the quilt top, batting, and backing.

2. Quilt the layers.

3. Join binding strips and bind the raw edges.

Quilt assembly

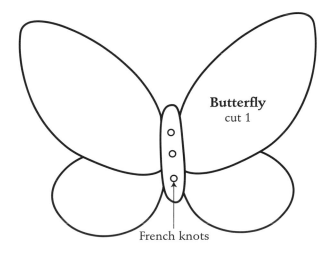

Butterfly
cut 1

French knots

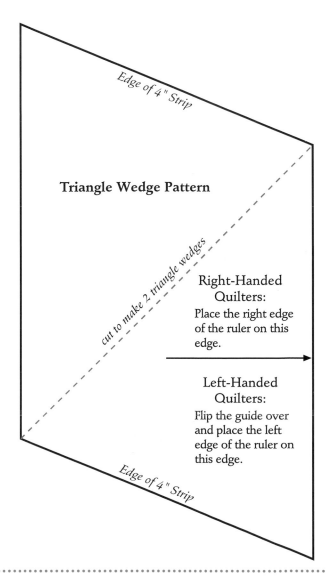

Triangle Wedge Pattern

Edge of 4" Strip

cut to make 2 triangle wedges

Edge of 4" Strip

Right-Handed Quilters:
Place the right edge of the ruler on this edge.

Left-Handed Quilters:
Flip the guide over and place the left edge of the ruler on this edge.

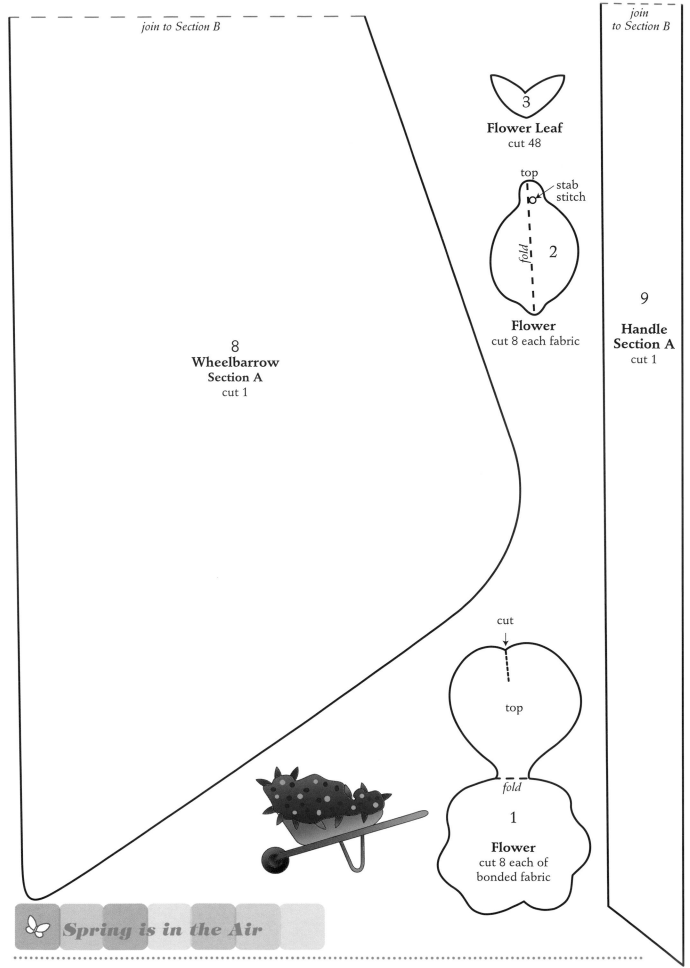

3

Flower Leaf
cut 48

top

stab
stitch

fold

2

Flower
cut 8 each fabric

8
Wheelbarrow
Section A
cut 1

9

Handle
Section A
cut 1

cut

top

fold

1

Flower
cut 8 each of
bonded fabric

Spring is in the Air

3 Quilters Celebrate the 4 Seasons
Karen Combs, Bethany S. Reynolds & Joan Shay

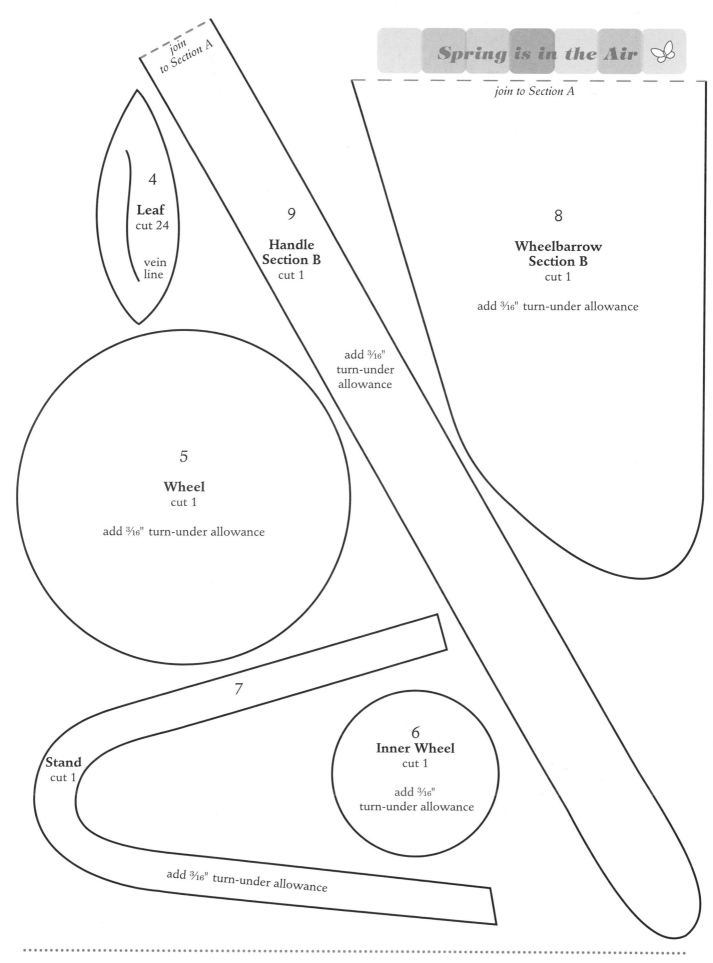

join
to Section A

join to Section A

4
Leaf
cut 24

vein
line

9

**Handle
Section B**
cut 1

8

**Wheelbarrow
Section B**
cut 1

add ³⁄₁₆" turn-under allowance

add ³⁄₁₆"
turn-under
allowance

5

Wheel
cut 1

add ³⁄₁₆" turn-under allowance

7

6
Inner Wheel
cut 1

add ³⁄₁₆"
turn-under allowance

Stand
cut 1

add ³⁄₁₆" turn-under allowance

3 Quilters Celebrate the 4 Seasons
Karen Combs, Bethany S. Reynolds & Joan Shay

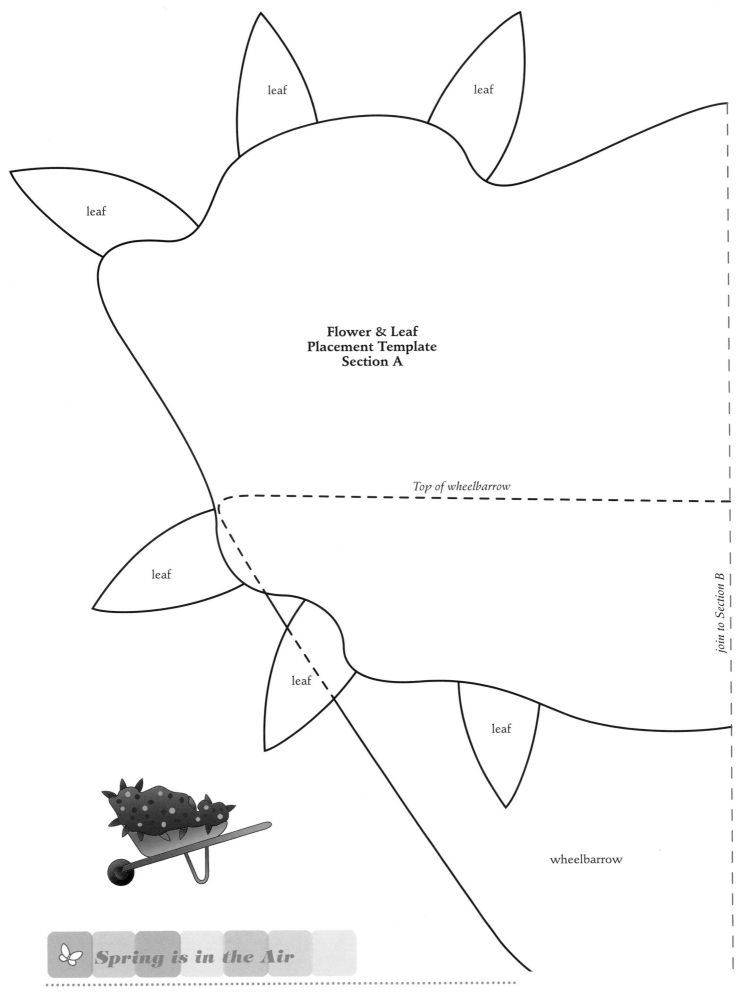

leaf

leaf

leaf

**Flower & Leaf
Placement Template
Section A**

Top of wheelbarrow

leaf

leaf

leaf

join to Section B

wheelbarrow

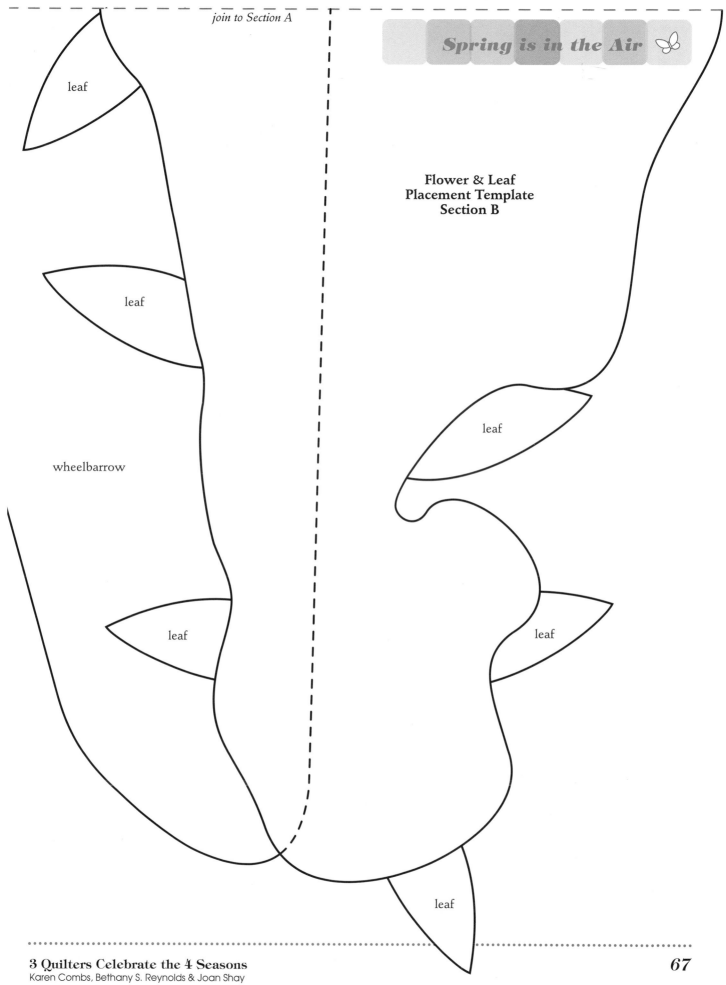

join to Section A

Flower & Leaf
Placement Template
Section B

leaf

leaf

leaf

wheelbarrow

leaf

leaf

join to Section A

leaf

May
Nosegays for Mother

Designed, pieced, and machine quilted by Bethany Reynolds. Bethany used Joan's Appli-bond technique to create three-dimensional sleeves to hold the Stack-n-Whack bouquets.

Before beginning, review the instructions for Stack-n-Whack (page 21) and for Appli-bond (page 17). Directions for NOSEGAY wall quilt begin on page 76.

Fabric Requirements

Measurements are in yards unless otherwise indicated.

If the design repeat of the **Flower Fabric** is:	6"–10"	11"–14"	15"–17"	18"–26"	over 26"
You will need this many yards for the Stack-n-Whack blocks:	3¾	2⅝	3⅛	4⅞	6 repeats

Additional Fabrics	Throw Quilt	Wall Quilt
White – background	2⅜	
Cream – background		⅞
Tan – accent fabric	⅝	
Green – nosegay sleeves	⅞	¼
Green – nosegay pieced block and Appli-bond leaves		⅛ of two
Pink – inner border	⅜	
Scraps – Appli-bond flowers		⅛ each of 3 colors for the flowers, scraps of yellow for flower centers
Outer border	½*	¼
Backing	3 (pieced crosswise)	⅝
Binding	⅝	¼

* The Flower Fabric yardage for the Stack-n-Whack technique includes the border. If you would like to use a different fabric, you will need a half yard, but don't reduce the Flower Fabric yardage.

Supplies

HeatnBond® UltraHold Iron-on Adhesive: throw quilt, 17" x ¾ yd.

NOSEGAYS FOR MOTHER THROW QUILT

Cutting the Flower Fabric

Prepare a 6-layer stack of the flower fabric following the instructions on page 21.

Stack-n-Whack Chart for NOSEGAYS FOR MOTHER
Cut layers 21" wide. Cut 6 identical layers.

If the lengthwise design repeat is:	Use this many design repeats:	Make this many stacks:
6" – 10"	2 repeats per layer	1
Over 10"	1 repeat per layer	1

Whack...	To Make...
(3) 2½" strips across the width	(18) 60° diamond block kits (6 per strip)*

*See p. 27 for instructions on cutting 60° diamonds.

Appli-Bond Appliqué

1. Cut the background and accent pieces, following the chart on page 71. To make a nosegay sleeve, cut one bonding piece 17" x 26". Bond the pair of fabric pieces. Cut four 4" x 26" strips from the bonded fabric. Cut (18) 4", 60-degree diamonds (page 27) from the strips.

2. To draw the stitching lines on the bonded fabric diamonds, mark a point 2¼" down from each side of one tip. Draw lines from each marked point to the other tip (Fig. 2–22).

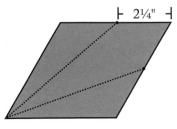

├ 2¼" ┤

Fig. 2–22

Cutting Background and Accent Fabrics

Position in Quilt	First Cut	Second Cut
White – small background triangles	(12) 2¾" strips across the width	(274) 2¾" 60° triangles (22 per strip)
White – large background diamonds in nosegay blocks	(3) 4½" strips across the width	(18) 4½" 60° triangles (6 per strip)
White – background diamonds in diamond Four-Patch units	(4) 2½" strips across the width	See Making the Setting Units section, step 2, page 73.
White – pieces A and B for setting	(2) 2⅞" strips across the width	See Making the Setting Units section, step 3, page 73.
White – piece C for setting	(1) 4¾" strip across the width	(12) 4¾" 60° triangles
White – top and bottom background fabric setting strips	(3) 2" strips across the width	
Tan – accent diamonds in diamond/triangle units	(4) 2½" strips across the width	(47) 2½" 60° diamonds (14 per strip)
Tan – accent diamonds in diamond Four-Patch units	(4) 2½" strips across the width	See Making the Setting Units section, step 2, page 73.
Green – nosegay sleeves	(1) 26" strip across the width	(2) 17" x 26" rectangles
Pink – inner border	(5) 1½" strips across the width	
Outer border	From the remaining flower fabric, cut (4) 2½" x 65" strips lengthwise. If you are using a different fabric, cut (5) 2½" strips across the width.	
Binding	(6) 2½" strips across the width	

*See p. 27 for instructions on cutting 60° diamonds and triangles.

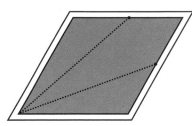

Fig. 2–23

Fig. 2–24

Fig. 2–25

Fig. 2–26   Fig. 2–27

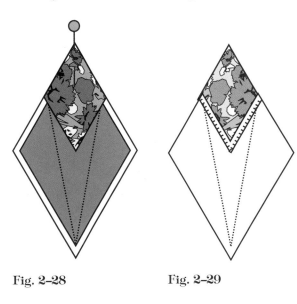

Fig. 2–28   Fig. 2–29

3. Center each bonded fabric diamond with the marked side up on a 4½" diamond of background fabric. Hold in place with tape or a dab of glue-stick, since pinning through the bonded fabric is difficult. Stitch on the marked lines (Fig. 2–23).

4. Cut (18) 2¾" 60-degree triangles (page 27) from the bonding material. Trim out a triangle from each, leaving an angled piece about ½" wide on each side (Fig. 2–24). These arrow-shaped pieces will be used to attach one flower fabric diamond to each nosegay sleeve during block construction.

Piecing the Nosegay Blocks

Piece 18 blocks as follows:

1. Lay out 1 block kit of 6 identical diamonds. Decide which end of the diamonds will be in the center, and place a pin in each at the center tip (Fig. 2–25).

2. Fuse an arrow-shaped bond piece to the wrong side of one diamond, lining it up with the tip opposite the pin (Fig. 2–26). With a rotary cutter and ruler, trim away ¼" from the 2 bonded edges (Fig. 2–27).

3. Place the diamond on a prepared nosegay sleeve, lining up the tips (Fig. 2–28). Fuse the flower fabric diamond in place. Machine appliqué the bonded edges using a stitch of your choice.

4. To reduce the bulk in the seams, turn the unit over and trim away the background fabric and bonded sleeve fabric (but not the flower fabric diamond) about ¼" from the appliqué stitching line (Fig. 2–29).

5. Sew 2 white small background triangles to each of the five remaining diamonds. Note that the triangles are sewn to the two sides opposite the pinned tip (Fig. 2–30).

6. Add a diamond/triangle unit to each side of the nosegay sleeve unit, taking care not to catch the edges of the bonded diamond in the seam allowances (Fig. 2–31). Piece together the 3 remaining diamond/triangle units (Fig. 2–32). Sew these 2 pieces together to complete a nosegay block. Fold the nosegay sleeve along the stitching lines and press as shown (Fig. 2–33).

Making the Setting Units & Pieces

1. Piece 47 diamond/triangle units, using one tan accent diamond and two small white background triangles for each (Fig. 2–34). Piece a unit to the top of each nosegay (Fig. 2–35). When the blocks are completed, 29 units (Fig. 2–34) will remain. Set these aside for now because they will be used in the quilt assembly steps.

2. Piece together a 2½" strip of white and a 2½" strip of tan. Make a total of four strip-sets. Press the seams toward the tan fabric. Cut the strip-sets at a 60-degree angle (page 27) to make (36) 2½" units (Fig. 2–36, page 74). Piece these units together in pairs to make 18 diamond Four-Patch units (Fig. 2–37, page 74).

3. From the 2⅞" strips of white background fabric, cut two triangles (piece B) and 12 half diamonds, piece A (Fig. 2–38, page 75). Use the template on page 74 to cut them.

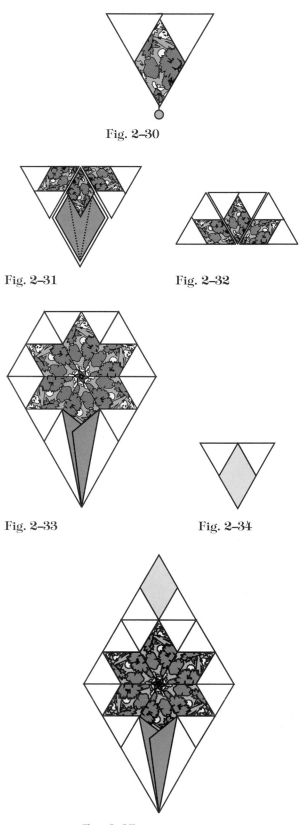

Fig. 2–30

Fig. 2–31   Fig. 2–32

Fig. 2–33   Fig. 2–34

Fig. 2–35

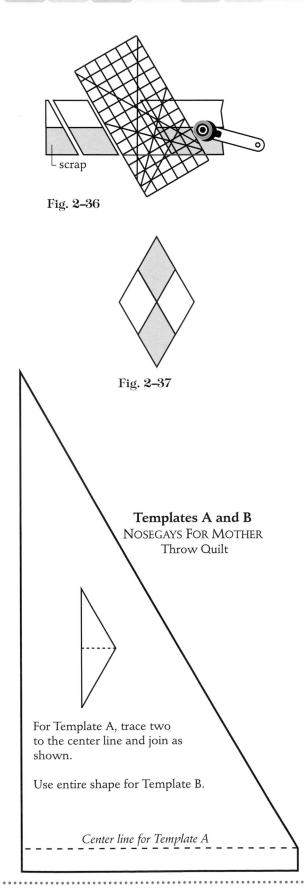

scrap

Fig. 2–36

Fig. 2–37

Templates A and B
NOSEGAYS FOR MOTHER
Throw Quilt

For Template A, trace two
to the center line and join as
shown.

Use entire shape for Template B.

Center line for Template A

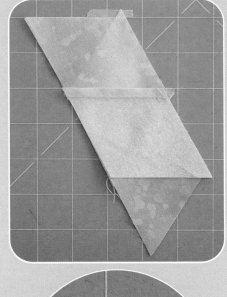

Karen's Diamond–Piecing Tip

Sewing diamonds can be tricky. They need to be offset by ¼" when sewn together. This can be a hard measurement to determine, but Karen has an easy way to offset the diamonds using ¼" masking tape.

Place a piece of ¼" wide masking tape along a line on your rotary mat. Place two diamonds right sides together and lay them on the edge of the tape (Plate 53). The white "tail" that sticks out at each end should measure ¼". Pin and stitch.

Plate 53. Stick the tape along a line on the mat and lay diamonds, right sides together, on the edge of the tape.

Assembling the Quilt

1. Follow the quilt assembly to arrange the nosegay blocks, setting units, and pieces A, B, and C. Piece together in sections to complete the diagonal rows. Join the rows.

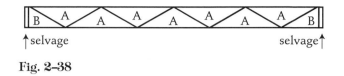

↑selvage   selvage↑

Fig. 2–38

2. Piece together the three 2" strips of the white top and bottom background fabric to make one long strip. Measure the quilt top across the center and cut two strips this length. Sew them to the top and bottom of the quilt.

Adding Butted Borders

1. Piece together the pink inner border strips to make one long strip. Measure the quilt top down the center, and cut 2 borders this length. Sew these borders to the sides. Measure across the width in the center of the quilt, and cut 2 borders this length. Sew them to the top and bottom.

2. If you use a fabric other than the flower fabric for your outer border, sew the strips together to make one long piece. Measure, cut, and sew the border strips to the sides and top and bottom as you did for the inner border.

Finishing

1. Curl the right side of the nosegay sleeves as shown on Plate 28 (page 18).

2. Cut the backing into two pieces each 1½ yards long. Sew them together along the long edges.

3. Layer the quilt top, batting, and backing. Quilt the layers.

4. Join the binding strips and bind the raw edges.

Quilt assembly

May

Nosegay Wall Quilt

Pieced and machine quilted by Bethany Reynolds. Appli-bond flowers designed and appliquéd by Joan Shay. Joan's cosmos blossoms and leaves fill in for the printed variety.

Before beginning, review the instructions for Appli-bond (page 17). Refer to the Fabric Requirements chart on page 69.

Cutting Background, Accent, Border, and Binding Fabric

Position in Quilt	First Cut	Second Cut
Green – nosegay pieced block	(1) 2½" strip across the width	(6) 2½" 60° diamonds*
Cream – small background triangles	(1) 2¾" strip across the width	(10) 2¾" 60° triangles*
Cream – large background diamond in nosegay block	(1) 4½" x 9" strip	(1) 4½" 60° diamond*
Cream – large background setting triangles	(1) 9¼" 60° triangle*	Cut up the center on the straight of grain to make 2 half-triangles.
Cream – small background setting triangles	(1) 5¼" 60° triangle*	Cut up the center on the straight of grain to make 2 half-triangles.
Cream – top and bottom background fabric setting strips	(1) 2" strip across the width	
Border	(2) 2½" strips across the width	
Binding	(2) 2½" strips across the width	

*See p. 27–28 for instructions on cutting 60° diamonds and triangles.

Supplies

HeatnBond® UltraHold Iron-on Adhesive, 17" x ¼ yd.

Embroidery floss: yellow and green

Appli-bond needle

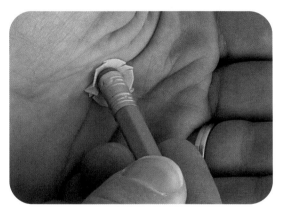

Fig. 2–39

NOSEGAY WALL QUILT

Appli-bond Appliqué

1. Cut the following:
- ❧ Green for nosegay sleeve: Cut 2 fabric pieces and 1 bonding piece 5" x 9".
- ❧ Green for Appli-bond leaves: Cut 2 fabric pieces and 1 bonding piece 3" x 7".
- ❧ Scraps for Appli-bond flowers. From each scrap, cut 2 fabric pieces and 3 bonding pieces 4" x 8".
- ❧ Yellow scrap for flower centers: Cut 2 fabric pieces and 1 bonding piece 1" x 2½".

2. Bond the fabric pieces together.

3. Trim the bonded nosegay sleeve piece to 4" x 9". Cut a 4", 60-degree diamond (page 27) from the bonded fabric.

4. Prepare templates for the flower, flower center, and the leaf (page 79). Trace the required number of pieces on each fabric as indicated on the pattern pieces. Cut out on the line (a seam allowance is not needed for Appli-bond).

5. To fringe the edges of the flower centers, draw a small circle in the middle of each flower center and cut to the marked circle (Fig. 2–39). Curl each center by heating with an iron for one to two seconds, cupping it in your hand, and shaping it around a pencil eraser. Hold until cool (Plate 54).

6. For each flower, layer and glue-baste two petal pieces, offsetting them as shown in Figure 2–40, and one center circle.

Plate 54

Fig. 2–40

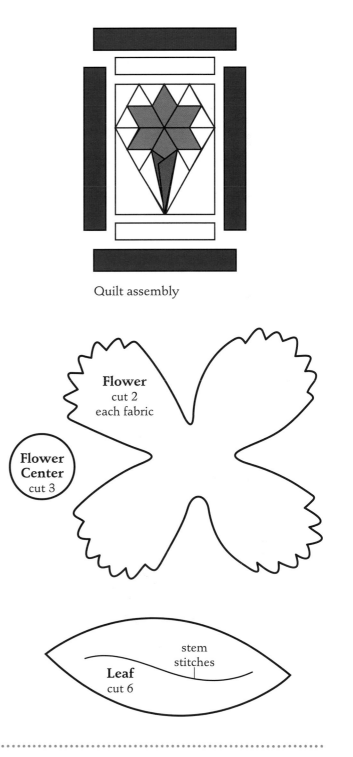

Piecing the Nosegay

For this step, you will use the instructions and figures for the throw quilt, substituting your green nosegay diamonds for the flower fabric diamonds. Follow steps two through four of the Appli-Bond Appliqué section (pages 70–72) and steps two through six of the Piecing the Nosegay Blocks section (pages 72–73).

Assembling the Quilt and Attaching the Appli-bond Pieces

1. Following the quilt assembly diagram, add the setting triangles to the nosegay block.

2. Measure the quilt top across the width and cut two strips this length from the background setting strip. Sew these strips to the top and bottom.

3. Measure down the center of the quilt top, and cut two border strips this length. Sew these strips to the right and left sides.

4. Measure across the width in the center of the quilt top, including the borders, and cut two borders strips this length. Sew the borders to the top and bottom.

5. Attach the leaves to the background with stem stitches (page 20) along the vein line (see leaf template on this page). Use 2 strands of embroidery floss and an Appli-bond needle.

6. To attach the flower, make four French knots (page 20) in the center of each blossom. Use two strands of yellow embroidery floss and wrap the needle 3 times.

7. Curl the right side of the nosegay sleeve as shown on Plate 28 (page 18). Curl the flowers and leaves by heating with and iron and folding over your finger. Hold each shape until cool.

Finishing

1. Layer the quilt top, batting, and backing.

2. Quilt the layers.

3. Join binding strips and bind the raw edges.

Quilt assembly

Flower
cut 2
each fabric

Flower Center
cut 3

Leaf
cut 6

stem stitches

June

Summer Star

Designed and machine pieced by Karen Combs. Machine quilted by Barbie Kanta. Intense colors found in a summer garden inspired this beautiful quilt. Gradations of color create an intriguing illusion of depth.

Summer Star

Fabric Requirements
Measurements are in yards unless otherwise indicated.

Light yellow – piece A	¼
Light gold – piece A	¼
Medium gold – piece B	⅜
Dark gold – piece B	⅜
Blue-green – piece C	¼
Raspberry – piece D	½
Medium gold and dark gold – first border	¼ of each
Raspberry – second border	⅜
Blue-green – third border	½
Backing	1¼
Binding	⅜

Cutting chart for SUMMER STAR on page 83.

Making the Blocks

MAKE 16 BLOCKS AS FOLLOWS:

1. Cut ends off the B and D pieces, using the 45-degree angle of a rotary ruler (Fig. 2–42, page 82). Set aside the trimmed corner from the B pieces; you'll use these triangles in the first border.

2. See Trimming and Matching Tricks (page 85). Sew the yellow A piece to the medium gold B piece, centering the A triangle on the B rectangle.

3. Sew the light gold A piece to the dark gold B piece, centering the triangle on the rectangle.

4. Sew the blue-green C piece to the raspberry D piece, centering the triangle on the rectangle.

5. Sew the units together (Fig. 2–41).

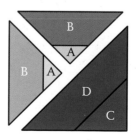

Fig. 2–41. Make 16.

left-handed   right-handed

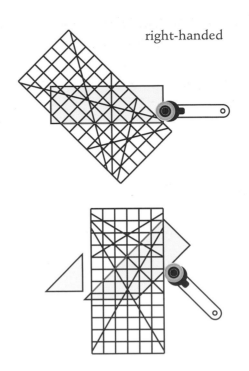

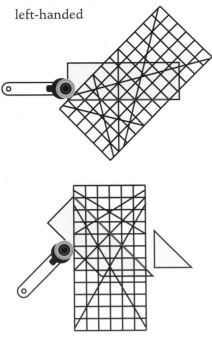

Fig. 2–42.

Fig. 2–43. Make 34.

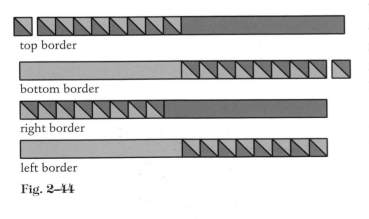

top border

bottom border

right border

left border

Fig. 2–44

Assembling the Quilt

Follow the quilt assembly diagram (page 84) for the following steps:

1. Arrange and sew the blocks in horizontal rows. Join the rows.

2. For the first border, which is free-form, use the triangles trimmed from the B pieces. Sew them together to form 34 half-triangle units (Fig. 2–43). Arrange 8 triangle units along each side of the quilt in a pleasing manner. Refer to the quilt assembly diagram, if needed. Sew the triangles together. Cut two 2⅛" x 14" medium gold strips and two 2⅛" x 14" dark gold strips. Add the strips to the ends of the triangle units. Add a corner unit to the top and bottom borders (Fig. 2–44).

3. Measure the quilt top down the center and cut one medium gold border unit and one dark gold border unit this length. Sew the borders to opposite sides. Measure across the

Cutting Chart for Block A		
Position in Quilt	**First Cut**	**Second Cut**
Light yellow – piece A	(4) 3¼" squares	Cut each square twice on the diagonal to make (16) quarter-square triangles.
Light gold – piece A	(4) 3¼" squares	Cut each square twice on the diagonal to make (16) quarter-square triangles.
Medium gold – piece B	(16) 2½" x 7¼" rectangles	See Fig. 2–42 (page 82)
Dark gold – piece B	(16) 2½" x 7¼" rectangles	See Fig. 2–42 (page 82)
Blue-green – piece C	(8) 3⅞" squares	Cut each square once on the diagonal to make (16) half-square triangles.
Raspberry – piece D	(16) 2⅝" x 9¾" rectangles	See Fig. 2–42 (page 82)
Medium gold and dark gold – first border	(2) 2⅛" strips across the width	See Assembling the Quilt, steps 2 and 3 (pages 82–83)
Raspberry – second border	(4) 2" strips across the width	
Blue-green – third border	(4) 3½" strips across the width	
Binding	2½" strips across the width	

width in the center of the quilt, including borders, and cut remaining borders this length. Sew them to the top and bottom of the quilt.

4. The second border is butted. Measure the quilt top down the center and cut two 2" raspberry border strips this length. Sew the borders to the sides. Measure across the width in the center of the quilt, and cut two 2" raspberry border strips this length. Sew the strips to the top and bottom of the quilt.

5. Measure, cut, and sew the third border strips as you did for the second border strips, using 3½" blue-green strips.

Finishing

1. Layer the quilt top, batting, and backing.

2. Quilt the layers.

3. Join binding strips and bind the raw edges.

Quilt assembly

Trimming and Matching Tricks

Centering a triangle on a trimmed rectangle can be difficult. There is an easy way to trim a triangle to match a trimmed rectangle.

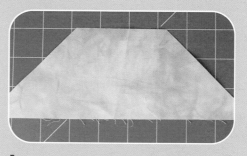

1. Fold the trimmed rectangle in half and crease with your finger.

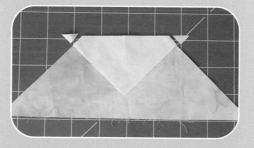

2. Fold the untrimmed triangle in half and crease with your finger.

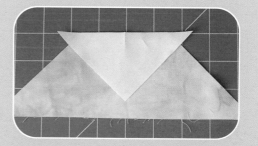

3. Match the center creases of the triangle and trimmed rectangle.

4. Carefully trim the edges off the triangle, matching the edges of the rectangle.

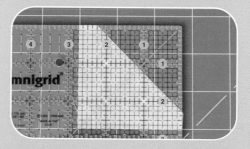

5. Measure the trimmed triangle with a ruler. This will serve as your measurement for trimming the other triangles.

Counterpoint Stars
Throw Quilt

Designed, pieced, and machine quilted by Bethany Reynolds.
Bethany's original design for the throw quilt is traditional in style,
but the Stack-n-Whack centers add drama to it.

3 Quilters Celebrate the 4 Seasons
Karen Combs, Bethany S. Reynolds & Joan Shay

Before beginning, review the fabric suggestions for Stack-n-Whack on pages 15–16. Directions for the wall quilt begin on page 91.

Fabric Requirements

Measurements are in yards unless otherwise indicated.

If the design repeat of the **Main Fabric** is:	6"–10"	11"–14"	15"–17"	18"–26"	over 26"
You will need this many yards for the Stack-n-Whack blocks:	2½	1⅞	2¼	3¼	4 repeats

Additional Fabrics	Throw Quilt	Wall Quilt
Light – pieces D, E, and G, and second border	1¼	
Red – piece C, and first border	1⅛	
Navy – pieces B, F, H, and I, and third border	2¼	
Light blue – pieces K and M		⅝
Medium blue – pieces N, R, and S, and border		⅝
Dark blue – pieces J and O		⅜
Medium red – piece L		¼
Dark red print – pieces P and Q		½
Backing	3½	1
Binding	¾	⅜

COUNTERPOINT STARS THROW QUILT
Cutting the Main Fabric

Prepare a four-layer stack of the main fabric, following the instructions on page 21.

Stack-n-Whack Chart for COUNTERPOINT STARS Throw Quilt
Cut layers 21" wide. Cut 4 identical layers.

If the lengthwise design repeat is:	Use this many design repeats:	Make this many stacks:
6" – 10"	2 repeats per layer	2
11" – 17"	1 repeat per layer	2
Over 17"	1 repeat per layer	1

Whack...	To Make...
(3) 5¼" strips across the width; whack (3) 5¼" squares from each strip and cut each square twice on the diagonal	(32) piece A block kits (12 per strip)

Fig. 2–45

Fig. 2–46

Piecing the Blocks

1. The Stack-n-Whack block kits (sets of four identical A pieces) are used for the centers of both Blocks 1 and 2. To piece one block kit, place two triangles right sides together and sew on the short bias edges. Make two pairs (Fig. 2–45). Sew the matching pairs together to make a square block center (Fig. 2–46).

2. Piece 80 B/C rectangle units. Join these with the block centers and D pieces to make 20 of Block 1 as shown in Figure 2–47.

3. Piece 48 E/F rectangle units and 48 C/G squares. Join these with block centers to make 12 of Block 2 as shown in Figure 2–48, page 90.

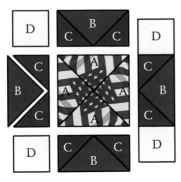

Fig. 2–47. Make 20.

3 Quilters Celebrate the 4 Seasons
Karen Combs, Bethany S. Reynolds & Joan Shay

Cutting Accent, Setting, Border and Binding Fabrics – Throw Quilt

Position in Quilt	First Cut	Second Cut
Light – piece D	(5) 2½" strips across the width	(80) 2½" squares (16 per strip)
Light – piece G	(2) 2⅞" strips across the width	(24) 2⅞" squares. Cut each square once on the diagonal to make (48) half-square triangles.
Light – piece E	(2) 5¼" strips across the width	(12) 5¼" squares. Cut each square once on the diagonal to make (48) quarter-square triangles.
Light – second border	(6) 2" strips across the width	
Red – piece C	(8) 2⅞" strips across the width	(104) 2⅞" squares. Cut each square once on the diagonal to make (208) half-square triangles.
Red – first border	(6) 2" strips across the width	
Navy – piece F	(4) 2⅞" strips across the width	(48) 2⅞" squares. Cut each square once on the diagonal to make (96) half-square triangles.
Navy – piece B	(3) 5¼" strips across the width	(20) 5¼" squares. Cut each square twice on the diagonal to make (80) quarter-square triangles.
Navy – piece I	(2) 12⅝" strips across the width	(4) 12⅝" squares. Cut each square twice on the diagonal to make (16) quarter-square triangles.
Navy – piece H	(2) 6⅝" squares from remainder of 12⅝" strips	Cut each square once on the diagonal to make (4) half-square triangles.
Navy – third border	(7) 2" strips across the width	
Binding	(7) 2½" strips across the width	

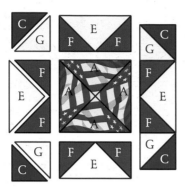

Fig. 2–48. Make 12.

Assembling the Quilt

1. Follow the quilt assembly diagram to arrange and sew diagonal rows of Blocks 1 and 2 and pieces H and I. Sew the rows together.

2. Piece together the first (red) border strips to make one long strip. Measure the quilt top down the center and cut the pieced strip into two border strips this length. Sew the strips to the sides of the quilt. Measure across the width in the center of the quilt and cut two borders this length. Sew them to the top and bottom.

3. Sew the second (light) border and third (navy) border in the same manner as you did for the first border.

Finishing

1. Cut the backing into two 1¾-yard pieces. Sew them together along the long edges.

2. Layer the quilt top, batting, and backing. Quilt the layers.

3. Join the binding strips and bind the raw edges.

Quilt assembly

July
Counterpoint Stars
Wall Quilt

Designed by Bethany Reynolds; color choices by Karen Combs. Pieced and quilted by Bethany Reynolds. Bethany asked Karen to give the design a different interpretation for the wall quilt. Karen used two shades each of blue and red to create the illusion of transparency. Before beginning, review Karen's fabric suggestions for Quilts of Illusion on page 13.

Cutting Accent and Setting Fabrics – Wall Quilt

Position in Quilt	First Cut	Second Cut
Light blue – piece K	(2) 2⅞" strips across the width	(18) 2⅞" squares. Cut each square once on the diagonal to make (36) half-square triangles.
Light blue – piece M	(2) 5¼" strips across the width	(12) 5¼" squares. Cut each square twice on the diagonal to make (48) quarter-square triangles.
Medium blue – piece N	(2) 2⅞" strips across the width	(18) 2⅞" squares. Cut each square once on the diagonal to make (36) half-square triangles.
Medium blue – piece R	(1) 5¼" strip across the width	(6) 5¼" squares. Cut each square twice on the diagonal to make (24) quarter-square triangles.
Medium blue – piece S	(4) 2½" squares from remainder of the R piece 5¼" strip	
Medium blue – border	(4) 1½" strips across the width	
Dark blue – piece J	(1) 2⅞" strip across the width	(14) 2⅞" squares. Cut each square once on the diagonal to make (28) half-square triangles.
Dark blue – piece O	(1) 5¼" strip across the width	(5) 5¼" squares. Cut each square twice on the diagonal to make (18) quarter-square triangles.
Medium Red – piece L	(2) 2⅞" strips across the width	(18) 2⅞" squares. Cut each square once on the diagonal to make (36) half-square triangles.
Dark Red – piece P	(1) 5¼" strip across the width	(5) 5¼" squares. Cut each square twice on the diagonal to make (18) quarter-square triangles.
Dark Red – piece Q	(2) 2⅞" strips across the width	(16) 2⅞" squares. Cut each square once on the diagonal to make (32) half-square triangles.
Binding	(4) 2½" strips across the width	

COUNTERPOINT STARS WALL QUILT

Refer to the Fabric Requirements chart on page 87.

Making Blocks and Border Units

1. Make five of Block 1 as shown in Figure 2–49. Make four of Block 2 as shown in Figure 2–50.

2. Make eight units as shown in Figure 2–51 and four units as shown in Figure 2–52.

Assembling the Quilt

1. Follow the quilt assembly diagram to arrange and sew the rows of Blocks 1 and 2. Sew the rows together.

2. Sew the 12 units together to make four inner border strips. Sew two of these to the sides of the quilt top. Sew an S piece to opposite ends of the remaining border strips. Sew these to the top and bottom.

3. Measure the quilt top down the center and cut two border strips this length. Sew the borders to two opposite sides. Measure across the width in the center of the quilt, including borders, and cut two border strips to this length. Sew them to the top and bottom.

Finishing

1. Layer the quilt top, batting, and backing.

2. Quilt the layers.

3. Join binding strips and bind the raw edges.

Fig. 2–49. Make 5.

Fig. 2–50. Make 4.

Fig. 2–51. Make 8.

Fig. 2–52. Make 4.

Quilt assembly

August

By the Sea

Designed and appliquéd by Joan Shay; machine quilted by Judy Irish. The sea is an integral part of Joan's life on Cape Cod, so it's no surprise she was inspired to make some Appli-bond fish! The seaweed is easy—you can twist it however you want, and with a few stitches to secure it, it sways with the tides.

Before beginning, review the instructions for Appli-bond on page 17.

Fabric Requirements

Measurements are in yards unless otherwise indicated.

Background fabric	1
Seashells, starfish, and seaweed	¼ each of 2
Long fish: Head, tail, fins 8–13, lower fin 1, upper fin 2, gills	⅛
Long fish: Upper fins 3–7	⅛
Long fish: Scales and foundation	¼
Long fish: Center round scales	⅛
Two round fish: Head, gills, and lower fins 10 and 11	⅛ each of 2
Two round fish: Upper and lower fins 2–4 and 5–9	⅛ each of 2
Two round fish: Scales and foundation	¼ each of 2
Two round fish: Tail 1	scraps
Small, medium, and large fish: Fabrics A, B, and C	⅛ each of 3, or scraps
Borders (cut [2] 5½" strips across the width) and binding (cut [4] 2½" strips across the width)	¾
Backing	1⅛

Supplies

HeatnBond® UltraHold Iron-on Adhesive: 2 yds.
Buttons for fish eyes: 3
Pebble beads for the small fish eyes: 2.5 mm in size (9)
Nylon beading thread: size D
Embroidery floss: green, tan, and colors to match the large fish heads
Appli-bond needle
Embroidery needle

Templates

Templates for the long fish are on pages 99–100; the round fish, pages 101–102; the small, medium, and large fish, page 103; and the starfish and seashells, pages 103–104.

Appli-bond Appliqué

To prepare for the following steps, make templates for each of the following: the long fish foundation (page 99), the long fish patterns (pages 99–100), the round fish foundation (page 101), the round fish patterns (pages 101–102), and the three small fish (page 103).

1. For the long fish, cut the following:
* ❧ Head, tail, upper and lower fins, and gills: Cut two fabric pieces and one bonding piece 4½" x 12".
* ❧ Fins 3–7: Cut two fabric pieces and one bonding piece 2" x 6".
* ❧ Scales, end scales, and foundation: Cut two fabric pieces and one bonding piece 7" x 17".
* ❧ Center round scales: Cut two fabric pieces and one bonding piece 2" x 12".

2. For each of the two round fish, cut the following:
* ❧ Head, gills, and lower fins 10 and 11: Cut two fabric pieces and one bonding piece 4" x 6".
* ❧ Tail 1: Cut two fabric pieces and one bonding piece 3" x 3".
* ❧ Upper and lower fins: Cut two fabric pieces and one bonding piece 3" x 10".
* ❧ Scales and foundation: Cut two fabric pieces and one bonding piece 8" x 17".

3. For the three small fish, cut the following:
* ❧ Fabric A: Cut two fabric pieces and one bonding piece 5" x 5".
* ❧ Fabric B: Cut two fabric pieces and one bonding piece 4½" x 9".
* ❧ Fabric C: Cut two fabric pieces and one bonding piece 3" x 3½".

Bond all the above fabric pieces.

4. Use your templates to trace the required number of pieces on the bonded fabrics. Cut them on the line. (A seam allowance is not needed for Appli-bond appliqué.)

5. Cut two fabric pieces and one bonding piece 8" x 12" for the seaweed. Bond the fabric pieces and cut into 20 strips ⅜" wide x 12" long.

LONG FISH

1. The long fish is assembled on its foundation before it is attached to the background. With matching thread and an Appli-bond needle, attach the pieces to the foundation with running stitches as indicated by the dashed lines on the template pieces (page 100). Slit the lower fin and attach pieces 1–13 in numerical order. Attach the tail end scales.

2. Following the shape of the foundation, start at the tail end and overlap slightly, attaching the scales to the foundation (Fig. 2–53, page 97) with stab stitches (page 20) as indicated on the scales. The topside of the fish has five small and seven large scales. The bottom edge has three small and nine large scales. Make sure the top scales end slightly under the head position

3. The round scales are attached through the center of the fish (Fig. 2–53). Start at the tail end and attach three each of the small, medium, and large round scales using stab stitches (page 20) and overlapping slightly.

4. Attach the gills on top of the round scale and slightly under the head position. Be sure to reverse one.

5. Position the head (a glue-stick will help hold it in place) and attach it to the foundation with French knots (page 20) where indicated. Use two strands of embroidery floss and wrap the Appli-bond needle three times.

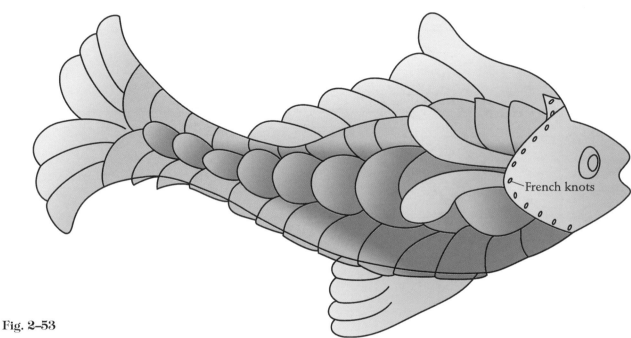

Fig. 2–53

French knots

ROUND FISH

1. Both round fish are assembled on their foundations before being attached to the background. To make the first one, thread the Appli-bond needle with a matching thread. Use stab stitches to attach the pieces to the foundation. The positions are indicated on the placement guide (page 101). Attach pieces 1–10 in numerical order.

2. For the scales, start at the base and overlap slightly following the shape of the foundation. Make sure the top row ends slightly under the head position.

3. Tuck the gills and lower fin 11 under the scales and attach with French knots (page 20). Use two strands of embroidery floss and wrap the Appli-bond needle three times.

4. Position the head (a glue-stick will help to hold it in place) and attach the head to the foundation with French knots (page 20). Use two strands of embroidery floss and wrap the Appli-bond needle three times.

5. Reverse the remaining round fish foundation and assemble it as above.

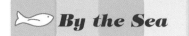
Attaching the Appli-bond Pieces

1. For the background, cut one piece 27½" x 30½".

2. Position the completed fish on the background. Raise several scales and attach the fish by stab stitching under the scales to the background. Be sure to attach them securely. Secure each head by sewing the eye button on the head, stitching through the background.

3. Attach the small fish in the upper right of the background with a stem stitch (page 20) along the curves within the body of each fish. Use two strands of embroidery floss and an Appli-bond needle. To attach each head, sew on a bead for the eye.

4. Because the seaweed is bonded, the strips can be twisted for a realistic look. Position groupings of three strips each and a group of 11 strips as shown in the photo of the quilt. Attach them with a stem stitch (page 20) through the center at each twisted area (Fig. 2–54). Leave a few of the group of 11 strips loose so they may extend onto the right side border.

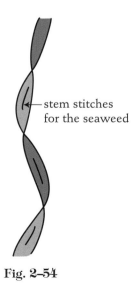

stem stitches for the seaweed

Fig. 2–54

Borders

1. Sew the border strips to the bottom and right edge of the quilt, stopping ¼" from the corner. Miter the border.

2. Make templates of the starfish and seashells (pages 103–104) and trace onto the seashell fabrics one nautilus shell, two starfish, two scallops, and two conch shells. Cut out, adding a ³⁄₁₆" turn-under allowance by eye.

Appliqué the shells to the borders in a pleasing arrangement, using the quilt photo as a guide. For the whelk and nautilus shells, appliqué the pieces in numerical order.

3. Embellish the starfish with French knots (page 20). Use two strands of embroidery floss and wrap the embroidery needle three times. The nautilus and scallop shells are embellished with stem stitches (page 20). For those, use two strands of embroidery floss and stitch where indicated.

4. Attach the loose seaweed strips onto the right side border with stem stitches.

Finishing

1. Layer the quilt top, batting, and backing.

2. Quilt the layers.

3. Join binding strips and bind the raw edges.

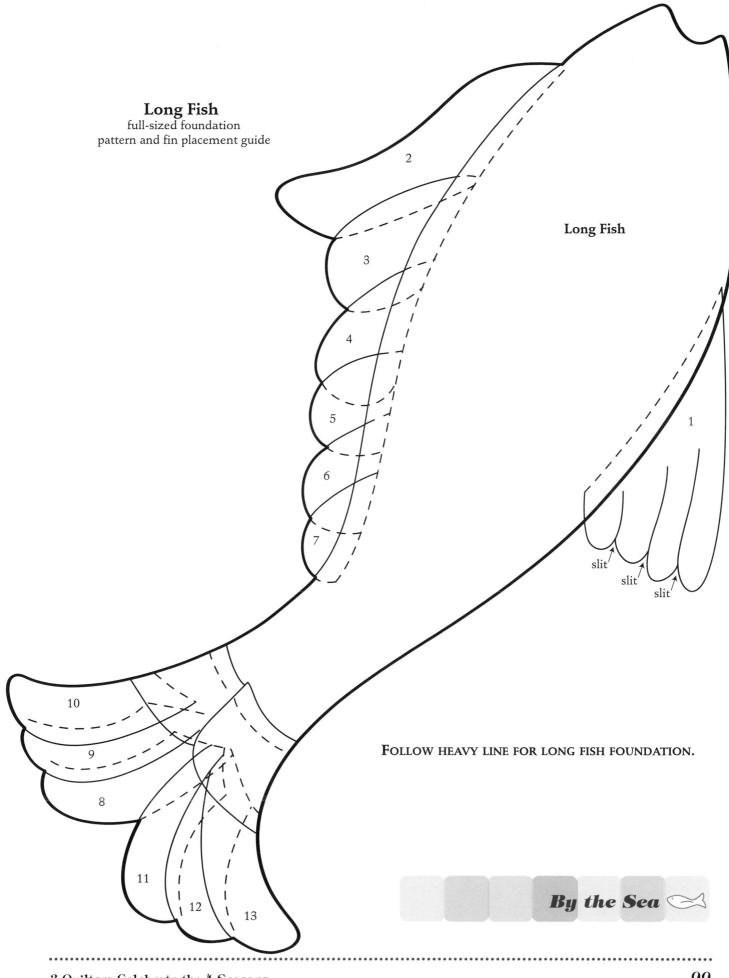

Long Fish
full-sized foundation
pattern and fin placement guide

Long Fish

2

3

4

5

6

7

1

slit slit slit

10

9

8

FOLLOW HEAVY LINE FOR LONG FISH FOUNDATION.

11

12   13

By the Sea

Long Fish Patterns

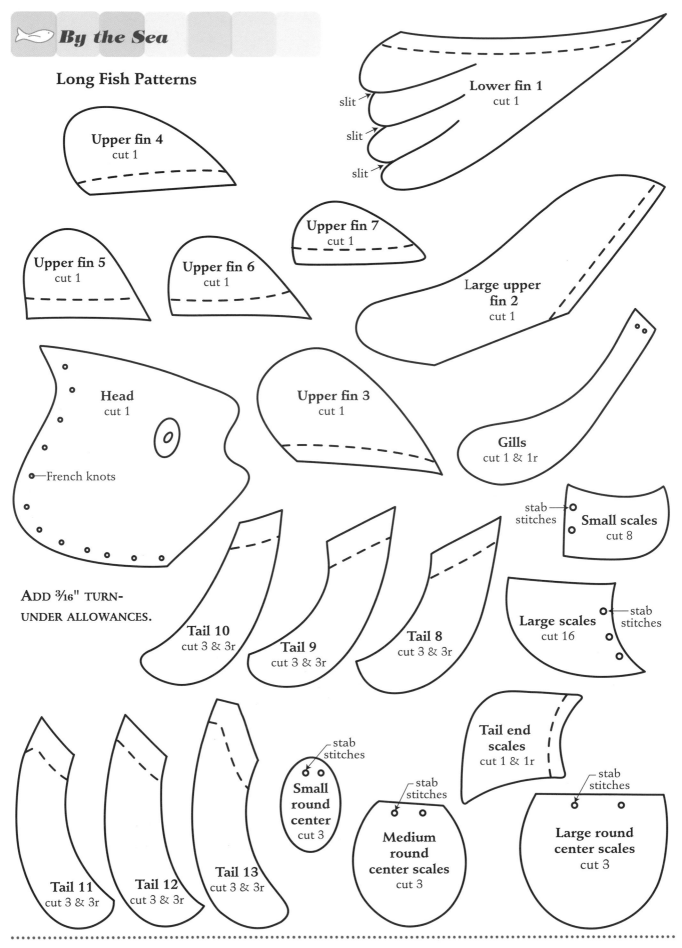

Upper fin 4
cut 1

Lower fin 1
cut 1

slit

slit

slit

slit

Upper fin 7
cut 1

Upper fin 5
cut 1

Upper fin 6
cut 1

Large upper fin 2
cut 1

Head
cut 1

French knots

Upper fin 3
cut 1

Gills
cut 1 & 1r

stab stitches

Small scales
cut 8

ADD ³⁄₁₆" TURN-UNDER ALLOWANCES.

Tail 10
cut 3 & 3r

Tail 9
cut 3 & 3r

Tail 8
cut 3 & 3r

Large scales
cut 16

stab stitches

Tail 11
cut 3 & 3r

Tail 12
cut 3 & 3r

Tail 13
cut 3 & 3r

stab stitches

Small round center
cut 3

stab stitches

Medium round center scales
cut 3

Tail end scales
cut 1 & 1r

stab stitches

Large round center scales
cut 3

Round Fish
full-sized foundation
pattern and fin placement guide

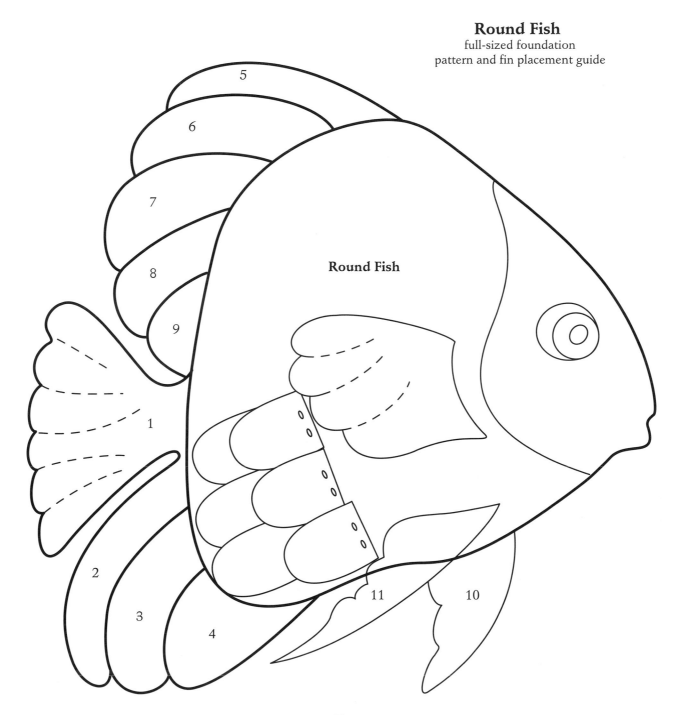

Round Fish

FOLLOW HEAVY LINE FOR ROUND FISH FOUNDATION.
CUT 1 AS SHOWN AND 1 REVERSE.

Round Fish Patterns

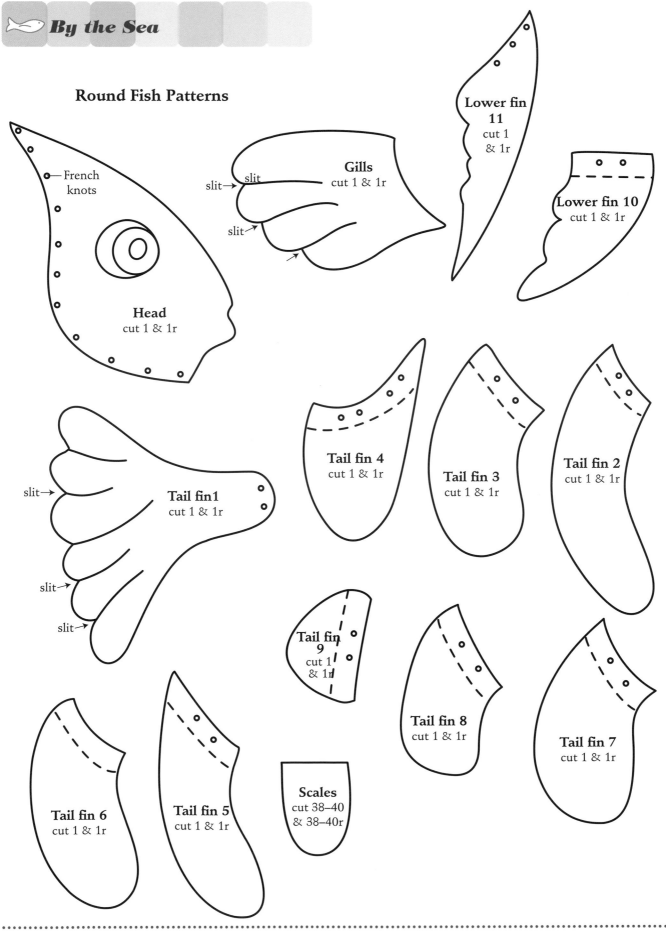

French knots

Head
cut 1 & 1r

Gills
cut 1 & 1r

slit

slit

slit

Lower fin 11
cut 1 & 1r

Lower fin 10
cut 1 & 1r

Tail fin 4
cut 1 & 1r

Tail fin 3
cut 1 & 1r

Tail fin 2
cut 1 & 1r

slit

slit

slit

Tail fin 1
cut 1 & 1r

Tail fin 9
cut 1 & 1r

Tail fin 8
cut 1 & 1r

Tail fin 7
cut 1 & 1r

Tail fin 6
cut 1 & 1r

Tail fin 5
cut 1 & 1r

Scales
cut 38–40
& 38–40r

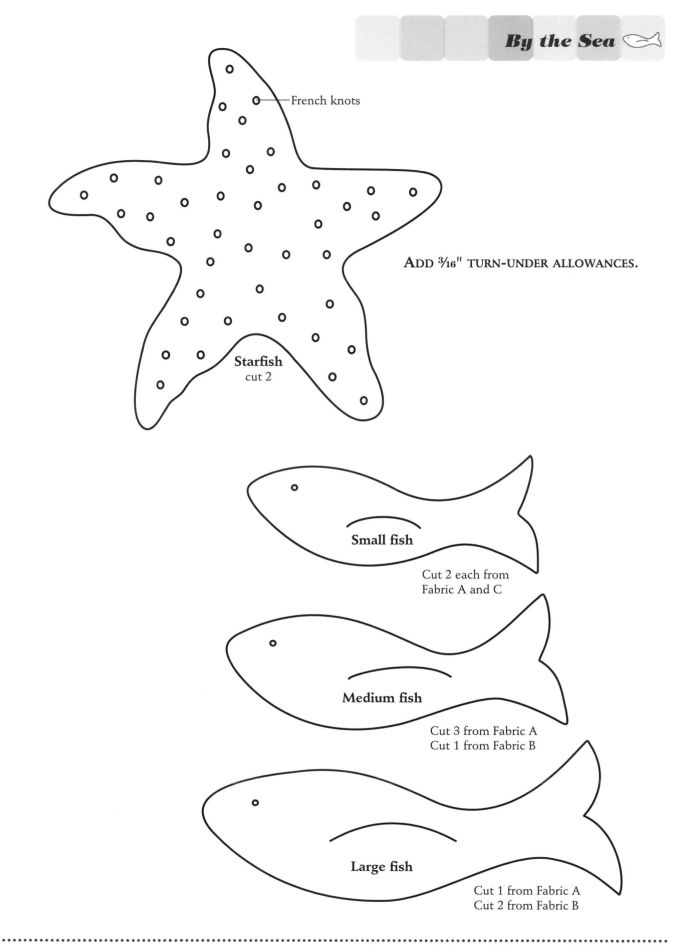

French knots

ADD ³⁄₁₆" TURN-UNDER ALLOWANCES.

Starfish
cut 2

Small fish

Cut 2 each from
Fabric A and C

Medium fish

Cut 3 from Fabric A
Cut 1 from Fabric B

Large fish

Cut 1 from Fabric A
Cut 2 from Fabric B

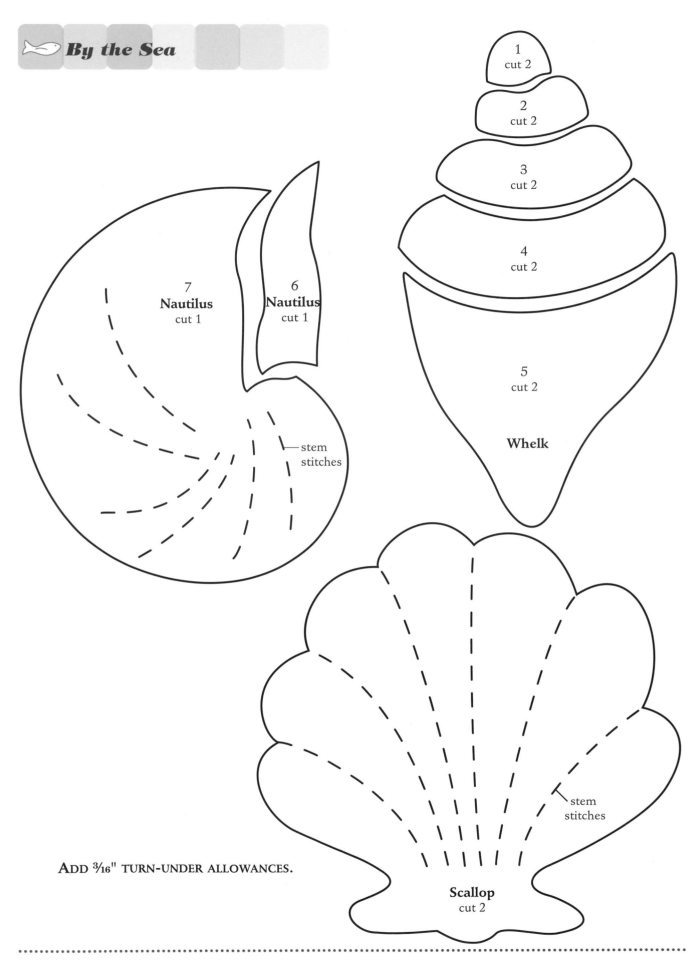

1
cut 2

2
cut 2

3
cut 2

4
cut 2

5
cut 2

Whelk

7
Nautilus
cut 1

6
Nautilus
cut 1

stem stitches

stem stitches

Scallop
cut 2

ADD ³⁄₁₆" TURN-UNDER ALLOWANCES.

3 Quilters Celebrate the 4 Seasons
Karen Combs, Bethany S. Reynolds & Joan Shay

September

Autumn Glow

Designed and machine pieced by Karen Combs. Machine quilted by Barbie Kanta. Let the colors of autumn fill your home with this beautiful quilt. The deep blue of the autumn sky, the green and red leaves of the Bradford pear tree, and the golden glow of the maple tree all inspired this quilt. The illusions of motion and transparency are added delights.

Fabric Requirements
Measurements are in yards unless otherwise indicated.

Ivory	1
Medium gold	7/8
Dark gold	5/8
Medium blue	1¼
Dark blue	2¼
Medium green	½
Cranberry red	¾
Backing	4
Binding	5/8

Cutting Chart for 13 Mosaic Blocks

Position in Quilt	First Cut	Second Cut
Medium Blue	(7) 4¾" strips across the width	(52) 4¾" squares
Cranberry red	(2) 4¾" strips across the width	(13) 4¾" squares
Dark blue	(3) 3⅞" strips across the width	(26) 3⅞" squares. Cut each square once on the diagonal to make 52 half-square triangles.
Dark blue	(3) 7¼" strips across the width	(13) 7¼" squares. Cut each square twice on the diagonal to make 52 quarter-square triangles.

Cutting Chart for 12 Star Blocks

Position in Quilt	First Cut	Second Cut
Medium green	(3) 3⅞" strips across the width	(24) 3⅞" squares. Cut each square once on the diagonal to make 48 half-square triangles.
Cranberry red	(3) 3⅞" strips across the width	(24) 3⅞" squares. Cut each square once on the diagonal to make 48 half-square triangles.
Ivory	(7) 3⅞" strips across the width	(72) 3⅞" squares. Cut each square once on the diagonal to make 144 half-square triangles.
Dark blue	(7) 3⅞" strips across the width	(72) 3⅞" squares. Cut each square once on the diagonal to make 144 half-square triangles.

Cutting Chart for Border and Binding Fabrics

Position in Quilt	First Cut	Second Cut
Dark blue	(1) 4½" strip across the width	(4) 4½" squares
Dark blue	(12) B pieces page 110	
Dark gold	(8) B pieces page 110	
Medium gold	(20) A pieces and (20) Ar pieces page 110	
Binding	2½" strips across the width	

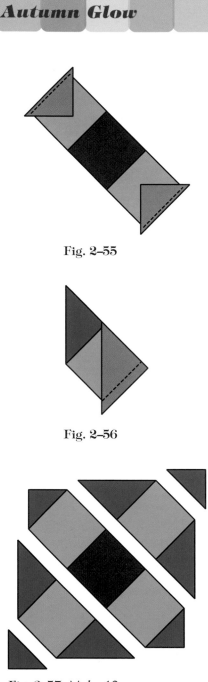

Fig. 2–55

Fig. 2–56

Fig. 2–57. Make 13.

Piecing the Mosaic Blocks

Make 13 mosaic blocks as follows:

1. Sew dark blue half-square triangles to the medium blue square, centering the triangles over the square. Trim the "dog ears." Repeat to make a second unit. Sew these units to either side of a red square (Fig. 2–55).

2. Sew two dark blue quarter-square triangles to a medium blue square, centering the triangles over the square (Fig. 2–56). Trim the "dog ears." Repeat to make a second unit.

3. Arrange and sew the units and dark blue half-square triangles together (Fig. 2–57).

Making the Pinwheel Star Blocks

Follow Fig. 2–58 on page 109 to make twelve pinwheel star blocks.

Making the Pieced Borders

1. Follow Figure 2–59, page 109, to make a pieced border. Repeat to make four.

2. Add a dark blue square to each end of two of the pieced borders (Fig. 2–60, page 109).

Karen's Template Cutting Method

For this method, make paper templates for the border patches A/Ar and B. Using a water-soluble glue-stick, dab glue on the bottom of a template. Lay the fabric on a rotary-cutting mat, right side up. Place the template on the right side of the fabric. The glue will make the template stay in place. Lay a rotary-cutting ruler on top of the paper template and line up the edge of the ruler with the edge of the paper template. Using a rotary cutter, cut around the paper template.

Assembling the Quilt

1. Following the quilt assembly diagram on this page, arrange and sew the mosaic and pinwheel star blocks in horizontal rows. Join the rows.

2. Sew the pieced borders to the quilt, first to the sides and then to the top and bottom

Finishing

1. Cut the backing into two-yard pieces. Sew them together along the long edges.

2. Layer the quilt top, batting, and backing. Quilt the layers.

3. Join binding strips and bind the raw edges.

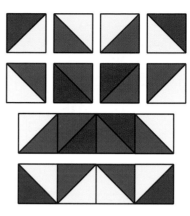

Fig. 2–58. Make 12.

Fig. 2–59. Make 4.

Fig. 2–60

Quilt assembly

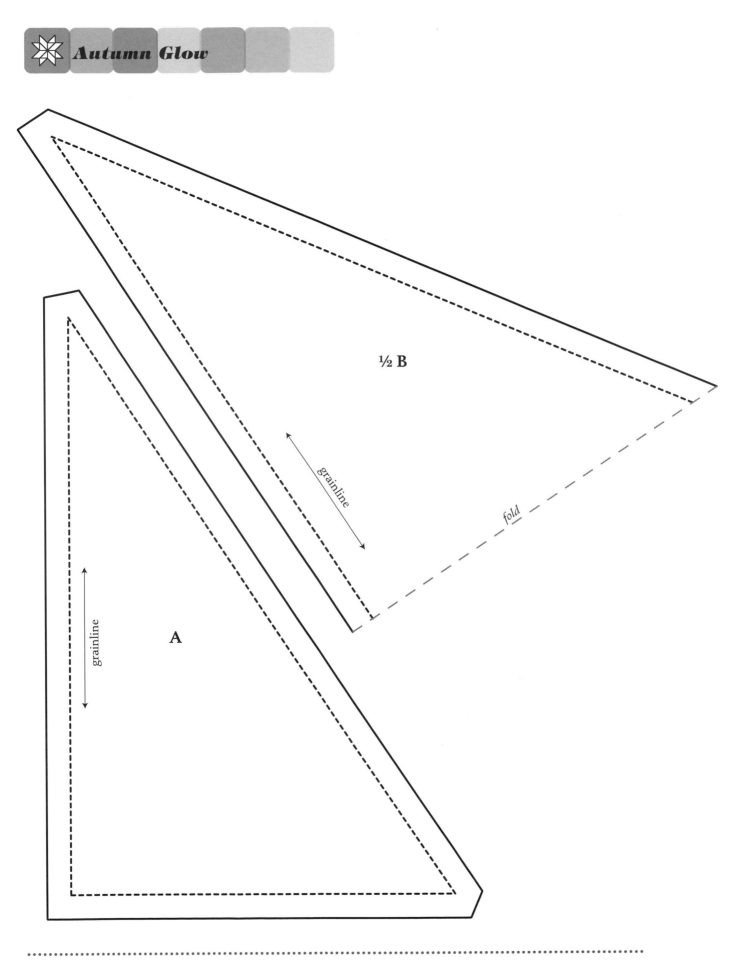

½ **B**

grainline

fold

grainline

A

October

Dancing Leaves *Throw Quilt*

Designed, pieced, and machine quilted by Bethany Reynolds. Bethany's throw quilt captures the kaleidoscopic effect of leaves on a crisp autumn day.

Skill level: **Average**
Finished block: **10" x 11½"**
Finished quilt: **62" x 75¼"**

Dancing Leaves

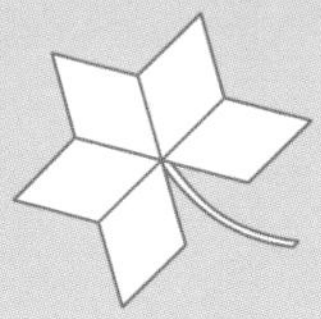

Before beginning the throw quilt, review the fabric suggestions for Stack-n-Whack on page 15. Directions for the wall quilt begin on page 118.

Fabric Requirements

Measurements are in yards unless otherwise indicated.

If the design repeat of the **Leaf Fabric** is:	7"–10"	11"–14"	15"–17"	18"–26"	over 26"
You will need this many yards for the Stack-n-Whack blocks:	3⅛	4⅜	2⅝	4	5 repeats

Additional Fabrics	Throw Quilt	Wall Quilt
Leaf fabric	1⅛ or equivalent in scraps (A 3" strip cut across the width will yield diamonds for 2 blocks.) (Note: this yardage is optional; omit if you use the Stack-n-Whack method.)	½ or 7 scraps each 3" x 21"
Background	3½ yds. of one fabric (For variety, ⅜–½ yd. each or 8 or more different fabrics. Blues and golds were used in DANCING LEAVES, page 111)	1½ (blue was used in DANCING LEAVES on page 117.)
Light, medium-light, and medium gold fabrics		⅝
Stem fabric	⅜	¼
Inner border	⅝	
Middle border		¼
Outer border*	1⅛	
Backing	4	2¾
Binding	⅝	½

* The Leaf Fabric yardage for the Stack-n-Whack version includes the border. If you would like to use a different fabric, this is the extra yardage you will need, but don't reduce the Leaf Fabric yardage.

Supplies

For fusible bias stems:
⅜" fusible bias tape making tool
1 roll ¼" fusible web tape

DANCING LEAVES THROW QUILT

Cutting the Leaf Fabric, Stack-n-Whack method

Prepare a five-layer stack of the leaf fabric, following the instructions on page 21.

Stack-n-Whack Chart for DANCING LEAVES Cut layers 21" wide. Cut 5 identical layers.		
If the lengthwise design repeat is:	**Use this many design repeats:**	**Make this many stacks:**
7" – 14"	2 repeats per layer	1
Over 14"	1 repeat per layer	1
Whack...	**To Make...**	
(4) 3" strips across the width	(21) 60° diamond block kits (6 per strip)	
*See p. 27 for instructions on cutting 60° diamonds.		

Cutting the Leaf Fabric, strip method

Cut 3" 60-degree diamonds following the instructions on page 27. Each of the 21 leaves has five diamonds, for a total of 105 diamonds.

Cutting Background Fabrics

Position in Quilt	First Cut	Second Cut
Small background triangles in leaf blocks	(11) 3¼" strips across the width	(210) 3¼" 60° triangles*
Large background triangles with stems, and setting triangles between blocks	(12) 5¾" strips across the width	(105) 5¾" 60° triangles*
Top and bottom setting half-triangles	(1) 6" strip across the width	(10) 6" 60° triangles*. Cut each triangle up the center to make pairs of half-triangles.
Inner border	(6) 2" strips across the width	
Outer border	From the remaining leaf fabric, cut (4) 5" x 69" strips lengthwise. If you are using a different fabric, cut (8) 5" strips across the width.	
Binding	(8) 2½" strips across the width	

*See p. 28 for instructions on cutting 60° triangles.
Note: If you are using a variety of fabrics for the background, as in the sample, cut the background triangles only as needed. For each leaf block, cut (10) 3¼" triangles and (1) 5¾" triangle.

Fig. 2–61

Preparing the Leaf Stems

1. From the stem fabric, cut an 11" strip across the width. From this strip, cut on the bias 11 strips ¾" wide.

2. Following the instructions with the tape maker, prepare the fusible bias strips. From each strip, cut two 6" lengths, for a total of 21 stem pieces.

3. For each block, place a bias strip on the 5¾" triangle of background fabric. Curve the strip slightly (Fig. 2–61) and fuse in place. Trim the excess stem fabric from the tip.

4. Machine or hand appliqué the bias strips.

Making the Leaf Blocks

Piece 21 blocks as follows:

1. Lay out one block kit of five identical diamonds. Decide which end of the diamonds will be in the center, and place a pin in each diamond center tip (Fig. 2–62).

2. Use one prepared stem triangle and ten small triangles of the same background fabric for each block. Join two small background triangles to each diamond, sewing them to the two sides opposite the pinned tip (Fig. 2–63).

3. Follow Figure 2–64 to complete a block.

Assembling the Quilt

1. Arrange the leaf blocks and setting triangles, using the quilt assembly diagram, page 116, for block and color placement. Sew the blocks and setting triangles and half-triangles into units.

2. Sew the diagonal seams in each vertical row. Sew the rows together.

Adding Borders

1. For the inner border, piece the strips to make one long strip. Measure the quilt top down the center and cut two borders this length. Sew the borders to two opposite sides. Measure across the width in the center of the quilt, including borders, and cut two borders this length. Sew them to the top and bottom.

2. If you are using an alternative border fabric, piece the strips to make one long strip. Measure, cut, and sew as for the first border.

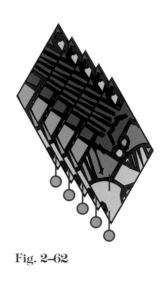

Fig. 2–62

Fig. 2–63

Fig. 2–64. Make 21.

Finishing

1. Cut the backing into two-yard pieces. Sew them together along the long edges.

2. Layer the quilt top, batting, and backing. Quilt the layers.

3. Join binding strips and bind the raw edges.

Quilt assembly

October
Dancing Leaves *Wall Quilt*

Designed, pieced, and machine quilted by Bethany Reynolds.
For the wall quilt version, leaves cut from a variety of scraps swirl
in front of one of Karen's three-dimensional cubes.

Before beginning the wall quilt, review Karen's fabric suggestions for Quilts of Illusion on page 13. Refer to the Fabric Requirements chart on page 112.

Cutting Background Fabrics		
Position in Quilt	**First Cut**	**Second Cut**
Leaf fabrics	(1) 3" x 21" strip for each block	(5) 3" 60° diamonds* from each strip
Light, medium-light, and medium golds – small background triangles in leaf blocks	(2) 3¼" strips across the width from each of 3 fabrics	24 each light and medium-light gold and 22 medium gold 3¼", 60° triangles*
Light, medium-light, and medium golds – large background triangles with stem and setting triangles	(1) 5¾" strip across the width from each of 3 background fabrics	6 each light and medium-light gold and 7 medium gold 5¾", 60° triangles*
Background large triangles (blue)	(2) 5¾" strips across the width	(12) 5¾", 60° triangles*
Background half-triangles (blue)	(1) 6" strip across the width	(6) 6", 60° triangles*. Cut each triangle up the center to make pairs of half-triangles.
Inner border	(4) 3" strips across the width	
Middle border	(4) 1" strips across the width	
Outer border	(4) 3" strips across the width	
Binding	(5) 2½" strips across the width	
*See p. 27 for instructions on cutting 60° diamonds and p. 28 for cutting 60° triangles.		

DANCING LEAVES WALL QUILT
Making the Leaf Blocks

Piece 7 blocks as follows:

    1. From the stem fabric, cut a 5" strip across the width. From this strip, cut on the bias seven ¾" strips.

2. Follow the steps in Preparing the Leaf Stems (page 114) to make seven fusible bias strips. Fuse the stems onto two light gold, two medium-light gold, and three medium gold large background triangles.

3. Make one each of the seven leaf blocks as in the quilt assembly diagram (Fig. 2–65).

Assembling the Quilt

1. Arrange the leaf blocks, setting triangles, and half triangles, using the quilt assembly diagram for block and color placement. Sew the blocks, setting triangles, and half-triangles into units.

2. Measure the quilt top down the center and cut two of the inner border strips this length. Sew them to the two opposite sides. Measure across the width in the center of the quilt, including borders, and cut two strips this length. Sew them to the top and bottom.

3. Measure, cut, and sew the middle border strips as you did for the inner border.

4. Measure, cut, and sew the outer border as you did for the previous borders.

Finishing

1. Cut the backing into two 1⅜-yard pieces. Sew them together along the long edges.

2. Layer the quilt top, batting, and backing. Quilt the layers.

3. Join binding strips and bind the raw edges.

Fig. 2–65. Quilt assembly

November
Thanksgiving Basket

Designed and pieced by Karen Combs. Appli-bond mums created and appliquéd by Joan Shay. Quilt layers machine quilted by Judy Irish. Karen's original design is based on her "combing through your scraps" technique. Karen asked Joan to work her magic with Appli-bond. Joan filled the basket with mums to create a very special wallhanging.

Thanksgiving Basket

Before beginning, review the instructions for Appli-bond on page 17.

Fabric Requirements

Measurements are in yards unless otherwise indicated.

Patchwork blocks	assorted light scraps and dark scraps
Appli-bond mums – petals	¼ yard each of 5 colors
Leaves	⅛ yard each of 3 colors
Light – inner border (cut [4] 1½" strips across the width) and setting triangles	¼
Dark – outer border (cut [4] 3" strips across the width	½
Backing	1⅛
Binding (cut 2½" strips across the width)	⅜

Supplies

HeatnBond® Ultra-Hold Iron-on Adhesive: 1⅔ yd.

Appli-bond needle

Embroidery floss: green

A narrow spool of thread for curling the petals

Glass beads: Size #6 (I used gold)

Nylon bead thread: green (size D)

Templates

The template for the leaf is on page 124, and the petals and flower centers are on page 126.

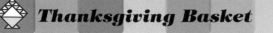
Combing Through Your Scraps

This quilt contains variations of the traditional Nine-Patch block: the Split Nine-Patch, Nine-Patches with all light fabrics, and Nine-Patches with all dark fabrics (Fig. 2-66).

As you select fabrics for the blocks, the color of the scraps does not matter. Any light or dark fabric may be used to create the blocks (for help with determining light and dark values, see page 11). The more variety in the scraps, the more colorful the quilt will be.

 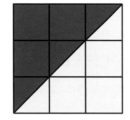 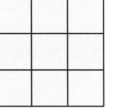 

Fig. 2–66. From left to right: traditional light and dark Nine-Patch, Split Nine-Patch, light Nine-Patch, dark Nine-Patch.

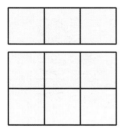

Fig. 2–67. Make 11.   **Fig. 2–68.** Make 3.

Piecing the Blocks

Make 10 Split Nine-Patch, 11 All-Light Nine-Patch, and 3 All-Dark Nine-Patch blocks as follows:

1. Cut 159, 2" squares from the light scraps and 87, 2" squares from the dark scraps.

2. Make 11 all-light Nine-Patch blocks (Fig. 2–67).

3. Make three all-dark Nine-Patch blocks (Fig. 2–68).

Collecting Scraps the Easy Way

There are several ways to collect the scraps for this quilt. If you have a large stash, you can sort through it, pulling out any light or dark scraps. However, if you don't have time to sort through your scraps, there is another option. Buy a watercolor packet at your local quilt shop or quilting catalog. A watercolor packet contains numerous 2" squares. You can make the patchwork blocks using the watercolor squares.

Many quilt catalogs and quilt shops also sell packets of 6" squares. This is an easy way to collect scraps for this quilt.

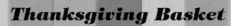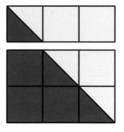

4. For the Split Nine-Patch blocks, use 30 light and 30 dark squares to create triangles as described in the sidebar. Make ten Split Nine-Patch blocks (Fig. 2–69).

Fig. 2–69. Make 10.

Quick Tip for Making 2" Triangles from 2" Squares

For the Split Nine-Patch blocks, there is a quick way to create triangles from squares.

Use a sharp pencil and a ruler to draw a line from corner to corner on a light square. Place a light and a dark square with right sides together (Fig. 2–70), aligning all edges. Sew on the pencil line (Fig. 2–71). Cut ¼" from the sewn line (Fig. 2–72).

Press the seam allowance toward the dark triangle.

There it is—a 2" triangle unit from two 2" squares (Fig. 2-73)!

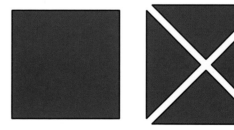

Fig. 2–70   Fig. 2–71   Fig. 2–72   Fig. 2–73

Assembling the Quilt

1. For the base of the basket, cut a 5¾" square from a dark fabric. Cut the square to make four triangles (Fig. 2–74). Two of the triangles will form the base of the basket.

2. For the side triangles, cut a light fabric into four 5¾" squares. Cut squares to make 16 triangles (Fig. 2–75). You will use 14 of these triangles.

3. Arrange the blocks and triangles as shown in the quilt assembly diagram, page 124. Sew the blocks and triangles into diagonal rows. Press seam allowances of alternating rows in opposite directions. Sew the rows together. Press the quilt top.

Fig. 2–74

Fig. 2–75

Quilt assembly

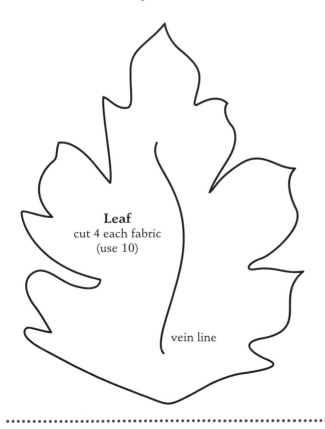

Leaf
cut 4 each fabric
(use 10)

vein line

Adding Butted Borders

1. For the inner border, measure the quilt top across the width in the center of the quilt, and cut two light 1½" border strips to this length. Sew the strips to the top and bottom. Measure the quilt from top to bottom through the center, and cut the two remaining strips to this length. Sew them to the sides.

2. For the outer border, measure the quilt top across the width in the center, and cut two 3" wide outer border strips to this length. Sew the strips to the top and bottom. Measure the quilt from top to bottom through the center, and cut the two remaining strips to this length. Sew them to the two remaining sides.

Appli-bond Appliqué for the Mums

1. Cut the following:
❖ Petals: Cut two pieces from each of the five petal fabrics and five bonding pieces 9" x 12".
❖ Leaves: Cut two pieces from each of the three leaf fabrics and three bonding pieces 4½" x 13".

2. Bond the fabric pieces for the petals and leaves.

3. Prepare templates for the petals, tracing only the darkened outline of each, the leaf (at left), and the circles (page 126). Use the templates to trace two large, two medium, and two small petals on each of the bonded petal fabrics. Trace four leaves on each of the bonded leaf fabrics (you will use only ten leaves). Cut on the line. (A seam allowance is not needed for Appli-bond.)

4. Use the small and medium/large center templates and a water-soluble marking pen to draw a circle in the center of each petal. Referring to the templates on page 126, the gray lines within each petal indicate the cutting lines. Cut each of your bonded petals as shown on the templates to create individual petals. Cut just to the drawn circles, but not into them.

5. Curl each petal by heating with an iron and shape it over a narrow spool of thread. Hold the shape until it is cool (Plate 55).

6. Heat two individual petals at a time and shape with your fingers to give them an irregular shape (Plate 56). Hold until cool. Repeat for all individual petals.

Attaching Appli-bond Pieces

1. Arrange the bonded leaves, in a pleasing manner, on the background and attach by embroidering along the vein lines. Use the stem stitch (page 20) with two strands of green embroidery floss and an Appli-bond needle.

2. Curl the leaves by heating them with an iron and crimping them with your fingers (Plate 30, page 19). Hold the shape until cool.

3. To make each mum, layer two large, two medium, and two small petals.

4. Attach the flower units to the background, where indicated, with five glass beads in the center of each mum. Use nylon beading thread and an Appli-bond needle.

Finishing

1. Layer the quilt top, batting, and backing.

2. Quilt the layers.

3. Join binding strips and bind the raw edges.

Plate 55. Heat each petal with an iron and shape it over a narrow spool of thread. Hold until cool.

Plate 56. Heat two petals and shape with your fingers. Hold until cool.

Small Petal
cut 2 each fabric

beads

Medium Petal
cut 2 each fabric

beads

**Thanksgiving Basket
Flower Patterns**

small
center

medium/
large
center

beads

Large Petal
cut 2 each fabric

December
Pieceful Holiday

Designed and appliquéd by Joan Shay. Machine quilted by Judy Irish. Wouldn't this wreath be a lovely addition to your holiday décor? Wired ribbon woven among the Appli-bonded leaves adds an especially elegant touch.

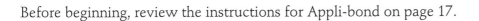

Before beginning, review the instructions for Appli-bond on page 17.

Fabric Requirements
Measurements are in yards unless otherwise indicated.

Background fabric	1
Green – holly leaves	¼ each of 10
Dark – poinsettia center petals	⅛
Light – poinsettia outer petals	¼
Backing	1
Binding (cut 2½" strips across the width)	⅜

Supplies

HeatnBond UltraHold Iron-on Adhesive: 2 yds.

Wire-edged ribbon: 1⅜" x 5 yds.

Glass seed beads: green, yellow, and red

Nylon bead thread: green and red (size D)

Appli-bond needle

Templates

Templates for the holly leaf and the center and outer petals are on page 131.

Appli-bond Appliqué

1. Cut the following:

❧ Green holly leaves: Cut two fabric pieces from each of the 10 colors and 10 bonding pieces 5½" x 17".

❧ Light outer petals: Cut two fabric pieces and one bonding piece 5" x 17".

❧ Dark center petals: Cut two fabric pieces and one bonding piece 2" x 17".

2. Bond the fabric pieces for the holly leaves and petals. Prepare templates for the holly leaves and poinsettia petals on page 131. Use the templates to trace 22 holly leaves from each bonded fabric, 21 center petals, and 24 outer petals. Cut on the line. (A seam allowance is not needed for Appli-bond.)

Making the Wreath

1. From the background fabric, cut one 30½" square. Draw a 16" diameter circle in the center of the background piece.

2. Position and attach the holly leaves to the background along the outer portion of the circle (Fig. 2–76). Leave about ¼" between the first points of the leaves. Place the tips on the drawn line. Attach each leaf with two green seed beads, using nylon beading thread and an Appli-bond needle. You will need approximately 56 leaves for the outer portion of the circle.

3. For the holly leaves in the inner portion of the circle, slightly overlap them (Fig. 2–76). Again, use two green seed beads, nylon beading thread, and an Appli-bond needle. You will need approximately 53 leaves for the inner portion of the circle.

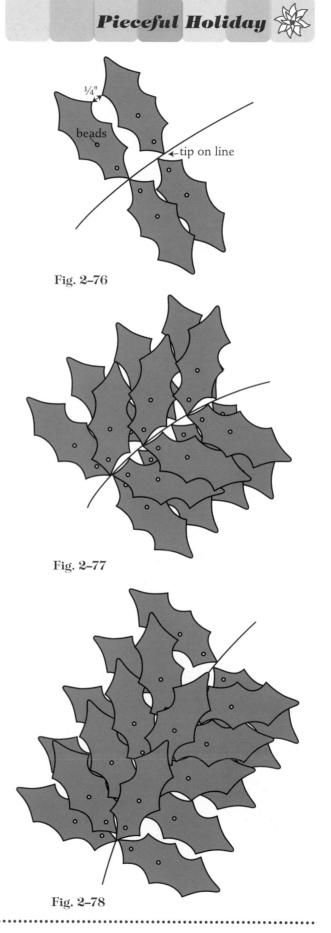

Fig. 2–76

Fig. 2–77

Fig. 2–78

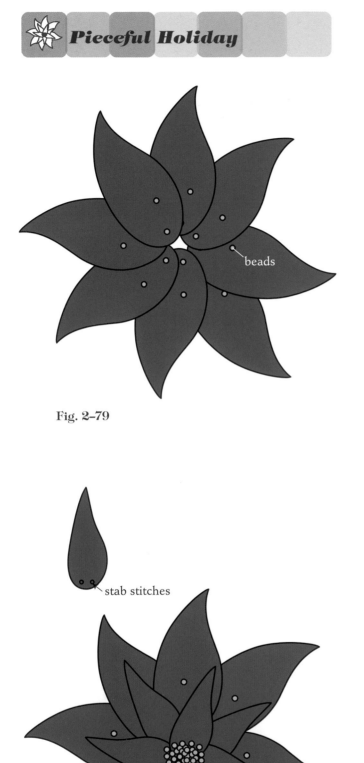

Fig. 2–79

beads

stab stitches

Fig. 2–80

4. Attach the second layer of leaves diagonally (Fig. 2–77). You will need approximately 42 leaves in the outer portion and 33 leaves in the inner portion.

5. Fill in with approximately 29 top leaves around the wreath (Fig. 2–78).

Making the Poinsettia Flowers

1. The poinsettias are attached to the wreath at approximately one o'clock, seven o'clock, and 11 o'clock positions, as shown in the photo of the quilt. For each poinsettia, position (Fig. 2–79) and attach eight outer petals to the wreath. Use two red seed beads, nylon bead thread, and an Appli-bond needle.

2. With stab stitches (page 20) placed in the positions shown, attach seven inner petals to the flower (Fig. 2–80).

To create the calyx, use a water-soluble marking pen to draw a small circle in the flower center, making sure that all inner petals are within the circle. Fill in the circle with yellow seed beads. Use red nylon bead thread and an Appli-bond needle.

Repeat for two more poinsettia flowers.

3. Curl the bonded poinsettia petals by heating with an iron and folding over your finger. Hold the shape until cool (Plate 29, page 18).

Attaching the Ribbon and Bow

1. Weave the ribbon around the wreath, occasionally catching it under a leaf. Hold it in place with a seed bead attached through the leaf and background.

2. Make a bow with the remaining ribbon. Attach it to the wreath at approximately the 4 o'clock position as shown in the photo of the quilt.

Finishing

1. Layer the quilt top, batting, and backing.

2. Quilt the layers.

3. Join binding strips and bind the raw edges.

Pieceful Holiday Patterns

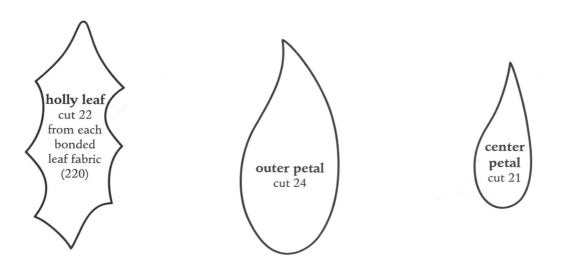

holly leaf
cut 22
from each
bonded
leaf fabric
(220)

outer petal
cut 24

center petal
cut 21

Group Quilt
Forget-Me-Knots

Designed by Bethany Reynolds, Karen Combs, and Joan Shay; pieced by Karen and Bethany; appliquéd by Joan; and machine quilted by Bethany. This quilt combines the talents of all three authors. Karen and Bethany designed the blocks while they waited in an airport café for their flights, and they trusted Joan to know what to do with the border when her turn came. The result is a first: an "Appli-bonded Stack-n-Whack Quilt of Illusion"! Forget-me-not flowers are a traditional symbol of friendship, so we believe the title is appropriate for a quilt that grew from the collaborative efforts of three good friends.

3 Quilters Celebrate the 4 Seasons
Karen Combs, Bethany S. Reynolds & Joan Shay

Before beginning the quilt, review Bethany's fabric suggestions for the Magic Mirror-Image Trick on page 16 and Karen's fabric suggestions for Quilts of Illusion on page 13. Also read Joan's instructions for Appli-bond on page 17.

Fabric Requirements

Measurements are in yards unless otherwise indicated.

If the design repeat of the **Main Fabric** is:	7"–10"	11"–14"	15"–17"	18"–26"	over 26"
You will need this many yards for the Stack-n-Whack blocks:	2½	3½	4¼	6⅜	8 repeats

Additional Fabrics	
Medium green – light box sides	½
Dark green – dark box sides	½
Dark blue – block corner triangles and borders	1⅝
Appli-bond blossoms*	¼
Dark green – Appli-bond leaves and vine	⅝
Medium green – Appli-bond leaves	¼
Backing	3¼
Binding	½

*Appli-bond blossoms may be cut from scraps of the Main Fabric.

Supplies

HeatnBond® UltraHold Iron-on Adhesive: ½ yd.

Embroidery floss: green and yellow

Appli-bond needle

Templates

Blossom and leaf templates for this project are on page 139.

Cutting the Main Fabric

Prepare an eight-layer stack of the main fabric, following the instructions on page 21.

Stack-n-Whack Chart for FORGET-ME-KNOTS

Cut layers 21" wide. Cut 8 identical layers for each stack.

If the lengthwise design repeat is:	Use this many design repeats:	Make this many stacks:
7"–10"	1 repeat per layer	2
Over 10"	1 repeat per layer	1

Whack...	To Make...
(3) 3" strips across the width; whack (7) 3" squares from each strip and cut each square once on the diagonal	(36) half-square triangle block kits (14 per strip)

Cutting Accent, Setting and Binding Fabric

Position in Quilt	First Cut	Second Cut
Medium green – light box sides	(6) 2¼" strips across the width	(36) 2¼" x 7" rectangles
Dark green – dark box sides	(6) 2¼" strips across the width	(36) 2¼" x 7" rectangles
Dark blue – borders	(4) 6½" x 50" lengthwise strips	See Assembling the Quilt section step 3, page 137.
From remaining width of fabric (approximately 16"), cut		
Dark blue – block corner triangles	(4) 2¼" strips across the width	(72) 2¼" squares (18 per strip)
Binding	2½" strips across the width	

Piecing the Blocks

Piece 36 blocks as follows:

1. To prepare the box sides, place a 2¼" square of dark blue fabric at one end of each medium and dark green box fabric rectangle, right sides together. Sew across the squares in the directions shown (Fig. 2–81). Trim the seam allowances to ¼" and press them as shown (Fig. 2–82).

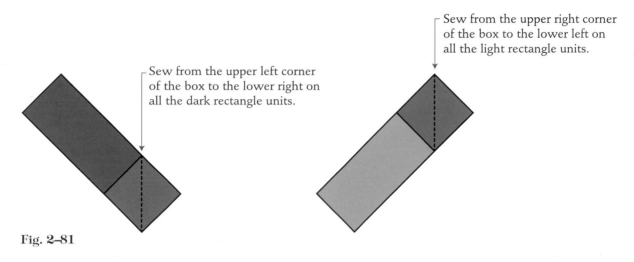

Sew from the upper left corner of the box to the lower right on all the dark rectangle units.

Sew from the upper right corner of the box to the lower left on all the light rectangle units.

Fig. 2–81

2. For each block center, you will need one block kit of eight identical triangles. The Magic Mirror-Image Trick (page 16) was used to create the blocks in this quilt. To use this effect, pair your triangles both right sides up rather than right sides together (Fig. 2–83).

3. Join the pairs by sewing the long bias edges together. For one pair of triangles in each block kit, stitch only halfway down, leaving the bottom half of the seam open (Fig. 2–84). Press the seam allowances to one side. Piece together the four squares as shown. The print motifs should match in the center. One corner will be open (Fig. 2–85, page 136). Clip the triangle tips that extend past the edges of the block.

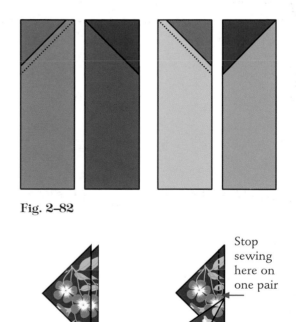

Fig. 2–82

Fig. 2–83

Fig. 2–84

Stop sewing here on one pair

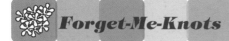

Fig. 2–85

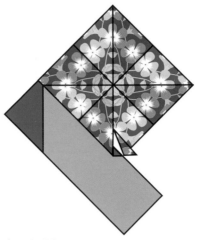

Fig. 2–86

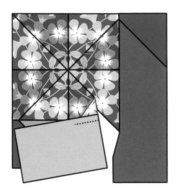

Fig. 2–87

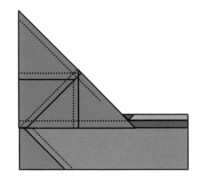

Fig. 2–88

Left-Handed

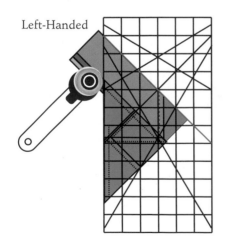

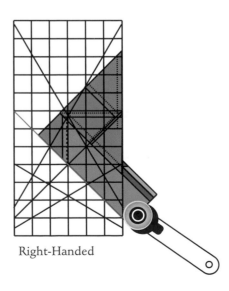

Right-Handed

Fig. 2–89

3 Quilters Celebrate the 4 Seasons
Karen Combs, Bethany S. Reynolds & Joan Shay

4. Sew a light green rectangle to the block as shown in figure 2–86. Finger-press the seam allowance toward the main fabric square. Sew a dark green rectangle as shown in figure 2–87. Finger-press the seam allowances toward the rectangle.

5. To finish the partial seam and join the rectangles with a mitered corner, fold the triangles flat as shown, with the seams nesting together and the straight edges together (Fig. 2–88). Trim the excess fabric from the box side rectangles to create a straight line along the bias edge. To do this accurately, place the edge of the ruler on the edge with the partial seam, and the 45-degree ruler line on the edge of the rectangular strip as shown (Fig. 2–89).

6. Finish sewing the partial seam and press the seam allowances to one side. Trim the triangle tips to complete the block (Fig. 2–90).

Assembling the Quilt

1. Lay out the blocks according to the quilt assembly diagram. Sew the blocks together in rows.

2. Sew the rows together to complete the center.

3. Measure the quilt from top to bottom through the center and cut two of the 50" border strips to this length. Sew these borders to the sides. Measure across the width in the center of the quilt, including borders, and cut the two remaining border strips to this length. Sew them to the top and bottom.

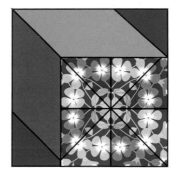

Fig. 2–90. Make 36.

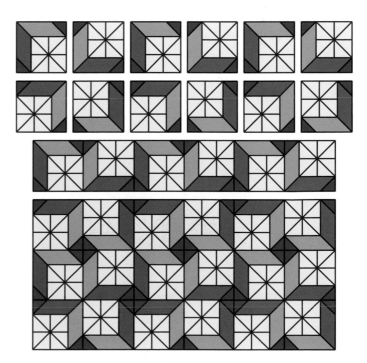

Quilt assembly

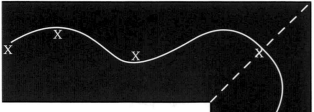

Fig. 2–91

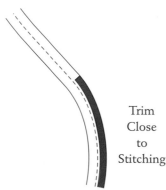

Trim
Close
to
Stitching

Fig. 2–92. If possible, for a curved bias stem, position the strip on the inside curve. Stitch down the center, trim the raw edge, turn and stretch the stem, and appliqué the outside curve.

Traditional Appliqué

1. The vine placement template is on page 140. To prepare the template, trace vine A on a sheet of paper and vine B on a second sheet. Tape A to B at the dotted lines. (Note: the border seam and corner placements are shown on vine B).

2. Transfer the vine markings to the upper right and lower left borders. Reverse the pattern and join at the corner to complete the vine (Fig. 2–91).

3. Cut a 15" x 30" strip from the dark green vine fabric. Cut six 1" bias strips to equal 112". Join the 1" bias strips to make two strips 56" long.

4. Fold one of the strips in half lengthwise, wrong sides together. Place the unfinished edge just beyond one of the marked lines in the border. Position the strip on the inside of the curve in the corner so it will stretch when it is folded and sewn (Fig. 2–92)

5. Using a small running stitch, sew through the center of the folded strip. Trim the unfinished edge close to the stitching. Turn the strip over the raw edge and appliqué it in place along the folded edge.

6. Repeat steps four and five for the other strip.

Appli-bond Appliqué

1. To prepare the Appli-bond, cut the following pieces:

- ❖ Blossoms: Cut two fabric pieces and one bonding piece 8" x 17".
- ❖ Dark leaves: Cut two dark fabric pieces and one bonding piece 3" x 17".
- ❖ Medium leaves: Cut two medium fabric pieces and one bonding piece 5" x 17".

2. Bond the fabric pieces for the blossoms and leaves. Using the blossom template, trace 126 blossoms on the bonded fabric and cut them out. Use the leaf template to trace 14 dark and 28 medium leaves on the bonded fabrics and cut them out. (A seam allowance is not needed for Appli-bond.)

3. Using a stem stitch (page 20), attach the leaves to the border where indicated by the "x" marks on the vine placement template (page 140). Each bouquet has three leaves, one dark and two medium. Use two strands of green embroidery floss and the Appli-bond needle.

4. Each bouquet has nine blossoms (Fig. 2–93) that are attached with one French knot (page 20). To make a French knot in the center of each blossom, use two strands of embroidery floss and wrap the Appli-bond needle three times.

5. To curl the blossoms, heat with an iron and rub your hand over them in a back and forth motion. For a photo of this "fluffing" technique, see Plate 31, page 19.

6. Curl the leaves by heating with an iron and folding over your finger as explained on page 18 of the general instructions. Hold the shape until cool.

Finishing

1. Cut the backing into two 1⅝-yard pieces. Sew them together along the long edges.

2. Layer the quilt top, batting, and backing. Quilt the layers.

3. Join binding strips and bind the raw edges.

Fig. 2–93

Forget-Me-Knots Patterns

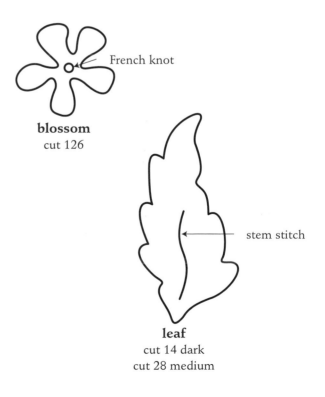

French knot

blossom
cut 126

stem stitch

leaf
cut 14 dark
cut 28 medium

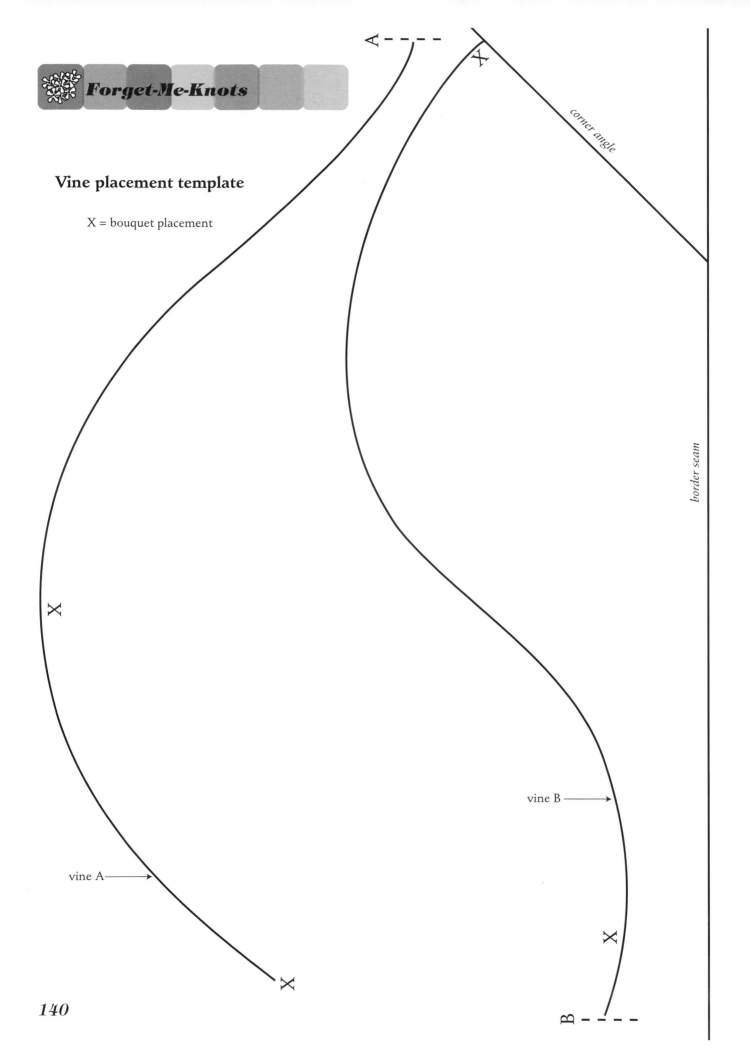

Forget-Me-Knots

Vine placement template

X = bouquet placement

A

X

corner angle

border seam

X

vine B ⟶

vine A ⟶

X

X

B

BlockBase software, The Electric Quilt Company, 1991–2002.

Combs, Karen. *Optical Illusions for Quilters.* Paducah, Kentucky: American Quilter's Society, 1997.

——. *Combing Through Your Scraps.* Paducah, Kentucky: American Quilter's Society, 2000.

——. *Floral Illusions for Quilters.* Paducah, Kentucky: American Quilter's Society, 2003.

Electric Quilt 5 software, The Electric Quilt Company, 1991–2002.

Reynolds, Bethany S. *Magic Stack-n-Whack® Quilts.* Paducah, Kentucky: American Quilter's Society, 1998.

——. *Stack-n-Whackier Quilts.* Paducah, Kentucky: American Quilter's Society, 2001.

——. *Magic Quilts by the Slice.* Paducah, Kentucky: American Quilter's Society, 2003.

Shay, Joan. *Petal by Petal.* Paducah, Kentucky: American Quilter's Society, 1998.

——. *Petal Play the Traditional Way.* Paducah, Kentucky: American Quilter's Society, 2001.

STASH software, The Electric Quilt Company, 1991–2003.

Yamin, Pat. *Look What I See.* ASN Publishing, 2001.

Supplies & Resources

BSR Design, Inc.
P.O. Box 1374
Ellsworth, ME 04605
Web site: www.bethanyreynolds.com
Quilting supplies (including Stack-n-Whack® rulers)
and workshops and lectures by Bethany Reynolds

Connecting Threads
13188 NE 4th Street
Vancouver, WA 98684
360-260-8900
1-800-574-6454
Web site: www.connectingthreads.com
Quilting fabric and supplies (including Value Viewer)

eQuilter.com
Web site: www.equilter.com
Quilting fabric and supplies

Fire Mountain Gems
28195 Redwood Highway
Cave Junction, OR 97523-9304
1-800-423-2319
Web site: www.firemountaingems.com
Beading tools and supplies

Hancock's of Paducah
3841 Hinkleville Road
Paducah, KY 42001
1-800-845-8723
Web site: www.hancocks-paducah.com
Quilting fabric and supplies (including HeatnBond®)

Heartbeat Quilts
Helen Weinman
765 Main Street
Hyannis, MA 02601
800-393-8050
Web site: www.heartbeatquilts.com
Quilting fabric, kits, and supplies

J.T. Trading Corporation
P.O. Box 9439
Bridgeport, CT 06601-9439
203-270-7744
Web site: www.sprayandfix.com
Basting spray and wool batting

Karen Combs Studio
3021 Viewpointe Way
Columbia, TN 38401
Web site: www.karencombs.com
Quilting supplies (ValueViewer) and workshops and
lectures by Karen Combs

Petal Play
Joan Shay
102 Courtney Road
Harwich, MA 02645
508-430-0347
Web site: www.petalplay.com
Quilting supplies (including Appli-bond needles and
HeatnBond) and workshops and lectures by Joan
Shay

Quilt University
Web site: www.quiltuniversity.com
Online classes with national teachers (including
Karen Combs and Bethany Reynolds)

Roxanne International
295 West Louise Avenue
Manteca, CA 95336
1-800-993-4445
Web site: www.thatperfectstitch.com
Glue-Baste-It™ appliqué glue

The Stencil Company
28 Castlewood Drive
Cheektowaga, NY 14227
716-656-9430
716-668-2488 (fax)
e-mail: info@quiltingstencils.com
Web site: www.quiltingstencils.com
Quilting stencils

About the Authors

Karen, Joan, and Bethany are familiar to quilters for their numerous quilt books as well as their television appearances on HGTV's *Simply Quilts* and other popular quilt shows. All three travel extensively to teach and lecture for quilt guilds and conferences.

Karen Combs is known for her pieced quilt designs, especially her "Quilts of Illusion." Her designs encourage quilters to explore visual tricks like transparency, motion, and depth. Karen is a frequent contributor to quilting magazines. She is much in demand as a teacher who makes design concepts such as color easy and fun, even for artistically intimidated quilters. Karen lives in the rolling hills of Tennessee.

Joan Shay is an award-winning quilter from Cape Cod and the originator of the Appli-bond technique, an easy method for creating three-dimensional appliqué using bonded layers of fabric. Beginners enjoy instant success with this technique, and more experienced quilters appreciate the design opportunities it provides. Joan produces the Petal Play line of quilt patterns, kits, and supplies. She is an energetic and entertaining lecturer and teacher.

Bethany Reynolds is best known as the originator of Stack-n-Whack®, but her design interests don't stop there. She has a knack for finding ways to get great results with less work, and she loves sharing her tricks with quilters worldwide. At home on the coast of Maine, Bethany and her husband, Bill, produce a line of specialty rulers and patterns under their BSR Design Inc. label.

Other AQS Books

This is only a small selection of the books available from the American Quilter's Society. AQS books are known worldwide for timely topics, clear writing, beautiful color photos, and accurate illustrations and patterns. The following books are available from your local bookseller, quilt shop, or public library.

#6212   us$25.95

#5850   us$21.95

#4995   us$19.95

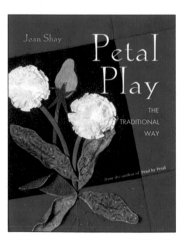

#5845   us$21.95

#5589   us$21.95

#5013   us$14.95

#6213   us$24.95

#4831   us$22.95

#5759   us$19.95